THE LIONESS UNCAGED

TAMAR NWAFOR

Breakfree Forever Publishing

Disclaimer

Author: Tamar Nwafor

ISBN: 978-1-916030190

Category: Abuse, Mental Health, Inspirational

The Inner Child

WARNING!

This book contains emotionally charged and challenging information around child abuse, sexual abuse, rape and other violence perpetrated against me. It tells the story of how I was – on a number of occasions – sexually, mentally, physically and emotionally abused from around the age of 5 years old, until well into my teens. You will read how these extreme traumas in my early years led me down a destructive and self-sabotaging path, but that's just where my story began – not where it ends.

You will learn that nothing is permanent, even for this traumatized little girl. She overcame her challenges, found herself, and now empowers many other women and girl survivors of domestic abuse and sexual violence, helping them to find *their* purpose and create fulfilling lives too.

Who is it for?

This book aims to give voice to the voiceless and hope to those who have been through similar circumstances; and have yet to see the light at the end of their tunnel:

- The woman who's taken all that life has thrown at her and is clinging onto the last few straws, as she anxiously awaits that breakthrough to her true happiness. The woman or girl who knows she's deeply unhappy, but is unaware that her perpetrator's behaviour isn't normal, and therefore doesn't identify what she's going through as abuse or violence. When she *does* try to speak up, she's shut down, called a liar and rejected from her home and community, while she watches in despair as everyone treats *him* as the victim. She doesn't know her true worth or the value of her flower, and so the impact of her childhood trauma continues to affect her adult life, making her vulnerable to re-victimization.

- The girl who is scared to tell anyone in fear of judgment, disbelief or rejection. The child who's scared and confused after having her life turned upside down, and doesn't have the words to express herself; she doesn't know what to do, who to believe, or if it will ever stop. The child who watches helplessly as her mother is regularly beaten up, desperately hoping and praying for it to end.

- The sister who fears that if she doesn't speak up, it may happen to her younger siblings too, and it will all be "her fault".

- The mother who doesn't know how to protect her little girl because she's been keeping the biggest secret of her life, hoping it doesn't happen to her child too. The mother who lives with guilt and rejection after losing her children because of his violence. The mother who tolerates his abuse because she believes that without him, she can't feed, clothe or provide a home for her children.

- The grandmother who 'sweeps everything under the carpet' in an attempt to avoid humiliation or embarrassment to her family, so she does exactly what *her* mother did and keeps quiet. By doing so, she's showing her daughter how to deal with these situations, as it's been done before her – continuing the cycle from one generation to the next.

These women and girls never received the support they needed. As a result, they blame themselves, believing it must have been their fault. It prevents them from forming healthy bonds with others, including their children, partners, friends, family and even coworkers. This in turn can affect their daily experiences, growth and contribution to society.

The overall impact can be vast, varied and complex, affecting all areas of their lives including their minds, bodies & spirits; education, employment/ career, financial, housing, parenting skills, sexual health and fulfilment, etc.

Within many groups of society, victims of abuse and violence often experience suicide and/or suicidal thoughts, homelessness, poverty, isolation, under educated or even miseducation. This leave them vulnerable to revictimisation, further affecting their progression in life. A side from the heavy burden victims generally have to bear – if they have children – they may also need to prove they're responsible parents or stand loosing their children to him, the State or some adoptive parents in the Family court system.

If, like me, you can relate to any of these circumstances, it may have also affected your confidence and self-esteem, or the value you place on yourself. You may lack knowledge of who you really are, impacting the way you perceive your inner and outer world. It can control your entire being, including the way you think, feel and react to situations.

Feeling powerless to your circumstances, you may believe that despite your best efforts, things don't always work out for you. Without knowing any different, you could end up settling for a life of pain, grief and constant reminders of your past, believing this is what life's all about. You sense something deep inside telling you there's more to life, but you're overwhelmed by the impact of your lived experiences. You feel stuck. Blinded. Confused. Anxious.

Fearful. Alone. Although you can't yet see the light shining brightly at the end of your tunnel, when you do, you will rise with a force like nothing anyone has ever seen before: The Lioness Uncaged.

Self-care

It's impossible for me to tell my story without it affecting others who may've also been traumatized, particularly in the first chapter of my book, where detailed and graphic accounts of the various abuse and violence I experienced is exposed. If you find reading my story causes you to have distressing flashbacks, I've listed a number of organizations at the back of the book where you can get help. You could also search online for other services near you. As you read this book, I'd also encourage you to reach out for support if you recognise you are in a domestic or sexually abusive environment.

Chapter 2 is about my family and I, immigrating to the UK to escape domestic abuse and child abuse, leading to years of self-sabotage including further abuse. Many people think that once you're physically away from the abuse, you're now ok and should get on with life as everyone else. What they don't understand is being away from the abuse creates another level of unknown challenges - added to those already mentioned; as you try to navigate your way through a new system that isn't necessarily designed to support or empower your recovery. As a result, you create many layers of masks to cope through your mental and emotional wellbeing and life challenges – making it even more challenging for anyone to see your true vulnerability or understand what your genuine needs are. Even when some may try to understand, we push them away, as we sink deeper into our own world of fear, denial, darkness and confusion.

If you make it to Chapter 3, you'll learn about some of the key challenges I faced around 'breaking the silence' at University. The last chapter of my book sets out my blueprint: 5 Steps to overcoming challenges '***The Lioness Way***'. It include lots of strategies and tools which has helped me to overcome the cycle of abuse and violence. It has also been tried and tested at my own support group, **The Lioness Circle** – as well as amongst my private clients.

Having overcome multiple sexual abuse and violence, neglect, bullying, gangs, and complex mental disorders, I am now a successful Businesswoman, Mentor, Coach, Author, Public Speaker, dedicated Mother and Home Educator. My daily work includes supporting and empowering women and young girls to break their silence in order to overcome abuse and violence and live the life they truly deserve.

To find out more about the work I do, and to get a free copy of my e-book '***The Lioness Guide to Self-Care***' please visit www.lionesstamar.com.

SCAN ME

CONTENT

FOREWORD

It's been proven within the field of psychology that childhood programming is at the root of whatever we experience as adults, both good and bad. Therefore, when seeking to get to the bottom of any challenges you're facing, the first place you should look is your childhood.

A child is subconsciously 'programmed' between the ages of 0-7, which is known as the 'imprint period' (this includes the unborn child). Anything a child is told or experiences repeatedly during this time goes deep into their subconscious mind, and becomes the program they run on for the rest of their life - or until they change it.

It's this subconscious programming that's responsible for the types of people, events or circumstances that we attract into our lives as adults.

For instance, if a child witnesses their mother being repeatedly beaten up by their father, they are more likely to either become an abuser themselves, or attract an abuser. If a child comes from a lineage of women who have been sexually abused, the chances of them experiencing sexual abuse is much higher. If a child never hears the words "I love you" and never feels loved, they will grow up emotionally detached, unable to give or receive true love.

If a child experiences extreme trauma (such as physical or sexual abuse) during their imprint period, the mind will disassociate and literally 'split', creating compartments in the mind, inorder to deal with the pain. They may not even remember the trauma as an adult, as it may be locked away in a part of the subconscious mind. But, as in Lioness Tamar's case, all it can take is a word, smell or touch to 'trigger' these memories and they can all come flooding back.

There's a stigma attached to sexual abuse within the black community, which means it's usually 'swept under the carpet'. Religion is merely a coping mechanism to deal with unresolved internal pain. Or we may attempt to patch up our life with temporary fixes such as food, pharmaceutical drugs, sugar, alcohol, smoking, or sex etc.

Instead of getting to the root cause of our issues, we merely look at the effect. This is like putting a plaster over a wound without first taking out what's causing the infection, hence the wound continues to get worse, becoming septic. To really heal from past trauma, we first have to admit that we're suffering. Many of us are still carry the trauma of our ancestors in our DNA, unaware of why we act and react in certain situations.

If we look at the BME community as a whole, we can see how the effects of slavery are still affecting us today. The acts of beating children mercilessly, child molestation and rape, negative affirmations, low self-esteem and a poor money mindset are a direct result of programming that has been passed down from the plantations, from one generation to the next. The most rebellious enslaved Africans were taken to the plantations in Jamaica in order to 'break them in'. They experienced the most brutal and barbaric treatment, to the point it altered their perception of themselves, and encoded within them a new way of being, contrary to their true, loving nature.

However, this generation is now breaking the cycle; Lioness Tamar is a fine example of a mother who has refused to pass the trauma down to her child, and in doing so, has helped to heal future generations. It's down to the mothers to heal from deep-seated psychological trauma so that our future generations stand a better chance. While I was editing Tamar's book 'The Lioness Uncaged', I felt so proud of her, knowing that despite her extreme trauma as a child, she has begun the process of changing her mental programming in order to break free from her generational cycle of abuse, and is healing from the psychological scars which she had carried into adulthood. Now, she's helping other women break their silence in order to heal too, and I pray that this will start a revolution that will ultimately help our whole community to heal; both the women and men. As Frederick Douglas said "Its easier to raise strong children, than to mend broken adults". Cezanne Taharqa

INTRODUCTION

Over the past 10 years I've spoken about much of my childhood abuse, but this is the first time I've gone into so much detail about the emotional neglect, violence, abuse, grooming and drug rape that I'd experienced. This is because up until now, I think a part of me still felt some misplaced level of blame, shame, anger and guilt. But not anymore...

Many people may question "Why now? Why am I ***digging up the past?*** Why can't I just let ***sleeping dogs lie?*** Why am I airing my dirty laundry in public?" They may blame my mother for not teaching me 'the right way', or my mother may even be blaming herself for the ***disgrace and humiliation*** I'm perceived to have brought upon the family.

I used to think it was too much to expect from my family and loved ones that if I opened up and told them all that I'd been through, they would be compassionate, understanding and believe me; that they wouldn't judge me and think it was all my fault, especially because I'm the ***common denominator*** in all these things I'm saying happened to me. I wanted them to sympathize and comfort me, not see me as I saw myself – like a disgusting disease eating away at their lives, that they'd rather not have to deal with.

Although some of my family and friends have been really supportive, I've learnt I was expecting too much from them, because they can't give me what I couldn't find within myself – ***my inner power!***

My Secret

What I didn't know is that ***the truth always comes out***. The more we try to hide it, the more it eats us up inside and takes us further away from who we really are. We can't run from our truth! We can try to hide, but only for a period of time before something happens outside our control that triggers it all off. But whether we try to hide it or tell everyone, people will always have something to say. If we keep our secret hidden, it can affect our core authentic self, affecting how we relate to others, and how others relate to and treat us. They may whisper behind our back, "Something's not quite right with her" or in the workplace they might say, "She doesn't represent our values." Wherever you are, you're being judged, and such judgement can have a profound effect on your life and add further baggage of injustice such as not getting that role, rejection from a potential partner or a breakdown in friendship circles. If we tell people our secret, their perception of us may change; they many think we're lying or that it was our fault. The thing is, we can't live our lives to please others, or hope that they may understand and give us what we need. Only we can do that for ourselves, once we find our inner strength and our light at the end of the tunnel.

I find that no-one will ever truly understand my trauma because they haven't experienced it in the way that I have. They haven't walked in my shoes or know how these experiences have affected me internally. People don't tend to understand what they can't see; they fear, undermine or disregard what they don't understand. The best thing anyone can do is listen, empathize and find out how they can help. I've also found that those who genuinely support us after we've shared our stories, are the ones that see our true value and believe in us, even when we don't believe in ourselves. These are the people we want to identify and have around us, as we continue down what can sometimes feel like a lonely road to overcoming challenges, finding our purpose and pushing forward on our journey to success. Having said that, it's important to manage our own expectations because our biggest fans can still become our greatest enemy.

I've chosen to write this book, not to seek revenge or intentionally make anyone feel uncomfortable (although no-one could blame me even if it does). This book is part of my personal healing journey, as well as to inspire other survivors to break their silence, in order to start or continue on their own healing journey.

I didn't realize how therapeutic it would be to allow myself to mentally re-live the finer details of my childhood – especially because I'd been running away from much of my past all my life. Although it didn't happen overnight, I've solidified my foundation and finally set my inner child free. I've healed that wounded child, so she's no longer stuck in a tragic past that haunts me every time I think about it.

Some of the details I've written about in this book had troubled me for years, causing severe illness to my mind, body and soul. I've experienced deeply-rooted mental illnesses such as suicidal thoughts, attempted suicide, night terrors, panic attacks, stress, anxiety, depression, post-traumatic stress disorder (PTSD), severe memory loss, personality and eating disorders.

These traumatic experiences had consumed my life and caused physical illnesses too, including chronic migraines, shallow breathing, chest pain, sleep disruption and deprivation, chronic muscle tension, vomiting, severe abdominal pain, STI's (sexual transmitted infections), womb/pelvic problems and a miscarriage. I was even told by a doctor that I wouldn't be able to have children – I'm so glad he was wrong!

Self-destruction

Combining the physical and mental impact with low self-esteem, confidence and self-worth, I've made countless 'bad' decisions; put my life at risk multiple times, including being part of street gangs; ended up in toxic relationships and situationships with people who didn't value me anymore than their last fix, who I cared for more than myself. This added further baggage to the weight on my shoulders; increased self-blame which reinforced my negative thoughts, beliefs, emotions and perception about myself and the world around me.

Self-healing

Such a self-destructive past is unsustainable. It forces you into a dark corner of extreme ***insanity***. Some never make it out alive, whilst others exist away their lives in a self-imposed prison, the new land of bondage and slavery. For me to be here sharing my story today, I'm evidence of the few that not only make it out alive, but also use their life experiences as a solid foundation to build a more successful and happy future. I've developed a true appreciation for all my life experiences. My happiness is no longer conditional to a particular thing or person, because it comes from within. My life has such true meaning now, and it doesn't matter who accepts or approves of me because I LOVE ME. With the tools I've developed, I'm confident in my abilities to bounce back from any situation as well as helping others to overcome their challenges too. I am a true asset to myself and my community with very unique experiences, and I wouldn't have it any other way.

I'm grateful for the fire that burns within me, and that self-determination to be free and happy inside, as I continue my journey of self-actualization. If it wasn't for the trauma I suffered as a child, I might not be on this journey, and therefore I wouldn't be the person I proudly am today.

Whilst I'm humbled, grateful and proud to have broken this mental and emotional cycle, I didn't do it on my own. I had spiritual guidance and support from others, that led me down paths where I was opened to accessing well-needed support such as mentoring, counselling and therapy. I believe that many more of us can overcome these challenges if we get the support we need, which is why I'm writing this book and have dedicated my life to empowering other women and girl survivors, particularly from the more disadvantaged backgrounds such as the black and minority ethnic (BAME) community.

Blocking It Out

As part of my coping mechanisms over the years, I tried so hard to block out much of my past. I thought that if no one talked about it, it would go away - but that's not true! What I didn't realize is that I was creating my own default settings that blocked out anything and everything that reminded me of what I'd been through. This included most of my childhood – the good, the bad and the indifferent.

I've had to come to terms with the fact that 'blocking it out' or not talking about 'it' doesn't mean 'it' didn't happen. 'It' still gets stored in our subconscious mind which can be abruptly brought to the surface of our consciousness by anything we see, hear, touch, taste or smell that reminds us of these past events.

Triggers

'A trigger is something that sets off a memory tape or flashback transporting the person back to the event of her/his original trauma. Triggers are very personal; different things trigger different people. ... A person's triggers are activated through one or more of the five senses: sight, sound, touch, smell and taste.' [1]

Being triggered can mentally bring us right back to that moment of the abuse, leaving us feeling scared, angry and helpless. As no-one wants to be triggered, we end up living our lives at the mercy of the trauma, hoping 'it' never re-surfaces.

But what do we do when a trigger hits us – as it's likely to? Have you been triggered before? How did you respond?

I learned to mask daily triggers as part of who I was, until that unexpected day in my Criminal Law class at Brighton University; my lecturer walked in and wrote on the blackboard in bold capital letters which he underlined, while verbally announcing "Today's lecture is about **RAPE!**" In that moment, everything came flooding back to me all at once! I experienced all three of the body's automatic response to threat: Flight, Fight and Freeze [2]. I physically froze in my chair whilst my mind was flooded with flashbacks of negative images and thoughts operating at over 100 miles per hour. My mind was full of chaos and became a war zone! I sat there unable to move, leave, or hear what he was saying. At the end of the lesson, I was the first one out the door. I ran so fast down the corridor with no specific destination in mind, just trying to get away "before anyone finds out." Although it would've been the most natural thing at the time for me to go home and overdose on drugs and alcohol,

1 https://psychcentral.com/lib/what-is-a-trigger/
2 https://www.nwbh.nhs.uk/healthandwellbeing/Pages/Fight-or-Flight.aspx

thankfully, I ran straight to my university counsellor and that was my saving grace – my turning point – the start of my conscious healing journey. Up to now, I still can't explain why I chose to go there, apart from the understanding that my higher self knew I was ready to face my core challenges. Since then, my life as I knew it has never been the same.

Memory Loss

Blocking out my past had a huge effect on my ability to remember things; big or small, good or bad, and this includes both short-term and long-term memory. In protecting us, the brain doesn't pick and choose which aspects of past experiences to block out – it aims not to remember things we don't want to, which includes anything associated with the experience – whether we're aware of it or not.

The more traumatic the experience, the more memory we stand to lose.

As a result of my abuse starting so early in my childhood and lasting for many years, I have little or no memory of what I was truly like, pre-abuse years. Writing this book has forced me to remember finer details surrounding my early years, which has helped me pieced together and fully embrace who I was before the abuse, and how it affected my life. It feels like I'm now painting my picture on a blank canvas – except the canvas was my dark and empty space inside, and the picture is my treasured memories, both good and bad. I now have much more confidence about who I am, which has helped me to create a solid foundation within, and reclaim much more of my power that was stolen from me. I'm so grateful to be in a much healthier mindset, so remembering and writing about my past doesn't traumatize me anymore. Instead, it uplifts and empowers me.

By writing this book, I hope to inspire and empower others to break their silence and free themselves of mental and emotional baggage from traumatic experiences. By doing so, we can start our healing journey, improve our wellbeing and become who we're truly meant to be.

"None but ourselves can free our minds."

~ Marcus Garvey

DEDICATION

This book is dedicated to my son Zion Nwafor. You've been a massive inspiration behind my continued growth, and I hope that one day you may come to understand and share your own story, the story of your mother and that of our people. You're a natural born leader and I'm truly grateful you chose me to be your mother.

I'm thankful for all the support I've received from those who have helped me along the way, including my mother, siblings, extended family and friends, teachers, mentors, coaches, colleagues, business partners, other survivors at **The Lioness Circle** and my therapist Maya. I'm also very grateful for technology and how easily accessible I've been able to find and share knowledge including self-healing tools.

CHAPTER ONE

My Early Years
Challenges of Child Abuse

Sandy Bay

I was around five years old when we moved to Sandy Bay, Jamaica. It was a small community, with built-up houses, and everyone knew everyone. The homes were built with wood, brick and water to each owner's requirements or affordability, and painted in whatever colours the owner chose. This gave the neighbourhood a bright and unique identity, especially when compared to houses in London. Most homes had at least two children with their mothers and grandmothers; some had their dads too.

My mother was a young vibrant and friendly woman, in her mid twenties. She'd recently moved away from our hometown in Salt Spring, Montego Bay, which looked very similar to Sandy Bay, but much busier. I remember moving there with my mother and my baby sister Joy, who was around two and a half years old. My big brother James remained in 'Mo-Bay' with my Aunt Patsy at this time, perhaps due to limited space. My mother would've had her four forth child by this time, though I can't remember having a baby with us until a few years later when my mother had her 5th child.

We were staying with a lady called Karen in her 2-bedroom house right next to the beach.

In Jamaica, out of respect, children were not allowed to call adults by their first name outright. We had to say 'Aunty' or 'Uncle', 'Mr', 'Miss' or 'Mrs'. So, although Karen was a stranger to me, my mother introduced her as 'Aunty Karen'.

Aunty Karen loved children, it's a shame she didn't have any of her own. She gave my sister and I many gifts including dolls and make-up. I was grateful to Aunty Karen for her kindness and I loved her for it, especially as we weren't accustomed to being spoilt like this. But I wasn't really into all those 'girly' things; as far back as I can remember, I've always been a 'tom-boy' – this is a name used in Jamaica to describe little girls who like to do 'boyish' things.

Cottage

In my own hometown in Cottage Bottom, Salt Spring, I used to enjoy playing rough with the boys; climbing trees (no matter how many times I fell off, hurt myself or promised my mother I'd stop). I loved going on adventure walks in the hills and gully of our land, and our neighbour's lands too. I enjoyed playing games outside and spending time alone, feeling free to do whatever I liked. It didn't help my 'tom-boyish' mindset that there were more boys than girls where I'm from.

Boys and girls

Boys were treated differently to girls, although I certainly didn't succumb to the well-known restrictions that allowed boys to go and do whatever they wanted, like freely going to play with their friends, whereas girls were expected to stay home and play with dolls (if they had any), or help with household chores.

If this taught girls how to become responsible women and mothers, then the boys were learning how to become irresponsible men, fathers and husbands. Without being consciously aware, we've facilitated the cycle of abuse; influencing the balance of power and control between the man and woman. We've also permitted our men to have lack of responsibility and accountability for their actions. Sadly, it was usually the mothers who taught their boys to be irresponsible, whilst the fathers reinforced lack of accountability with their absence. Of course, everyone was simply following the status quo and doing what ***they*** were taught. Most people don't do better because they don't ***know*** better.

No amount of beatings or punishment could stop me from going off with the boys. I would've preferred a game-boy over dolls and make-up any day. I remember my (late) cousin Junior who had a game-boy; I had some of the most fun times playing with him and his game-boy! My mother would complain all the time about how stubborn I was, saying I was always trying to get my own way. You can tell, I've always had a strong sense of determination and self-motivation to fulfil my desires from a young age!

My sister Joy loved all things girly, and so Karen would let her play dress-up with her make-up, hair products and even her clothes, shoes and purse. Nothing was off-limits for us. I'm sure Joy made a lot of mess in Aunty Karen's room, but she really didn't seem to mind. If anything, she found it funny and cute seeing Joy all dressed up in her clothes. I think she saw Joy as the little girl she had always wanted to have.

Moving to Sandy Bay, away from everything I knew, was a big change in my life; one that required a lot of emotional support to help me understand and adjust to this new life. However, my mother was busy sorting out our basic needs which was food, clothing and shelter; therefore, our emotional and mental needs were neglected.

The Sea

After the first few days of feeling alone and missing the things and people I loved, I decided to explore my new environment. I was drawn towards the sea which was right behind our house. I felt a sense of peace, calm and coolness on the beach, like something deep inside me was calling out to the water. I can remember throwing stones in the water to make ripples; finding seashells in the sand and searching for little creatures such as crabs and other creepy crawlies. I knew I wasn't allowed into the water by myself, but that didn't stop me wandering off on the beachside at my own will to play. I liked the cool breeze that met the boiling sun on my melanated skin, I could stay there for hours. It was like entering my own world where I could imagine anything I wanted to be. This became my favourite place in the whole world – and it often brought comfort to me when I felt sad or missed my friends and family from my hometown.

Although I didn't really have any friends at Aunty Karen's, I soon started to like living there. Each morning I'd wake up eager to go on a new adventure in my fantasy world by the seaside. One moment I was a pirate searching for buried treasure, next I was a princess warrior fighting the bad guys to protect the good, then I was the extraordinary Mighty Morphin Yellow Power Ranger – trying to save the planet from aliens! The possibilities were endless, and my imagination was my best friend. I can't believe how much fun I used to have on my own without any technology or electronic devices.

Tracey

But all of this drastically changed a few weeks later, when local gossip started about a young girl who lived next door to us. Her name was Tracey and she was about 14 years old. She lived with her mother and baby sister; they were one of the quietest families in the neighbourhood. Most times you would hardly notice they were home. Her mother worked long hours and Tracey was always under strict instructions whilst her mother was away. I imagine most evenings she was locked indoors looking after her baby sister and carrying out her mother's orders (i.e doing household chores).

One night, I heard Aunty Karen gossiping with some of the neighbours about Tracey meeting up with her boyfriend secretly. They said that when her mother was at work – she would sneak out of the house after putting her sister to sleep. As the adults continued to talk, I suddenly heard shouting coming from Tracey's home which I assumed was her mother beating her.

I felt so sorry for her that I started to pray;

"Dear Jesus, please help Tracey to be a good girl, listen to her mummy and not get herself into more trouble!"

I heard the neighbours say, "di next time dem ketch har a sneak out, there's no telling wat har madda ah guh do to har!" I later came to find out they weren't wrong.

Girl on Fire

"Child abuse is when anyone under the age of 18 is either being harmed or not properly looked after." [3]

Two weeks later, I was sitting on the beach engrossed in one of my adventures when I was distracted by a huge uproar coming from the front of the house. I ran towards the noise and saw a mob of people in Tracey's yard begging and pleading to Tracey's mother not to kill her, but neither Tracey nor her mother was anywhere to be seen. After listening to the adults talking, I figured out that Tracey's mother had left work early that day after being notified by one of the neighbours that they saw Tracey down the road with a man. Tracey's mother left work instantly and caught Tracey with the guy just as the neighbour had said. Apparently, Tracey's mother dragged her home in extreme anger and locked the door, so no one could get in or out. Suddenly, I heard Tracey screaming like never before. It was like she was on fire!

The neighbours tried to beat down the door, but no one could get in. Tracey's screams got worse with the banging and hitting sounds coming from inside the house. After about five to ten minutes the door opened and Tracey ran out, running and screaming erratically.

The neighbours tried to stop her to calm her down but at first nothing worked. I don't know if Tracey managed to say or give them some indication of what the problem was, or if the neighbours just figured it out, but I later saw two women holding Tracey's legs in the opposite direction under an outside tap so the water could wash her vagina. I wasn't allowed to get too close, so I couldn't see what else they did to help her, but I know that night Tracey

3 https://www.met.police.uk/advice/advice-and-information/caa/child-abuse/what-is-child-abuse/

slept at Dawn's house (one of the neighbouring women that helped her). I remember feeling very sad and scared for Tracey. I'd never seen anything like that before and still didn't know what her mother had done to her, until the following day when I heard Aunty Karen talking about it to one of the neighbours. She said "Tracey's madda 'pepper and salt' har vagina!" I felt even more disgusted and scared as my body tensed up in fear and anxiety. I remember thinking, "How can a mother do that to her own child?" I thought of Tracey's mother as a very wicked woman, and I no longer liked the fact that we were living so close to her.

Broken Trust: A Mother and Daughter's Relationship

'Child sexual abuse is a form of child abuse that includes sexual activity with a minor. A child cannot consent to any form of sexual activity, period. When a perpetrator engages with a child this way, they are committing a crime that can have lasting effects on the victim for years.' [4]

4 https://www.rainn.org/articles/child-sexual-abuse

A couple of months later we had to move again. I'm not sure what happened, but it didn't seem as if my mother and Aunty Karen fell out. I think it was just that we'd overstayed our welcome and it was simply time to move on. It seems Aunty Karen had agreed to put us up for a short period until my mother "got back on her feet", and five months seemed long enough.

My mother found new favour from another lady we called Aunty Kim who lived in Green Island – about a 20-minute drive from Aunty Karen's house. I remember feeling torn about leaving the peacefulness of the beachside, yet I was relieved to be moving away from Tracey's mother's house.

Green Island is another small community where everyone knows everyone. I didn't know of Aunty Kim until I met her when we were moving into her house. She lived in a small three-bedroom house with her boyfriend and three children – Kamar and Omar were around 7 and 5, while their baby sister was younger than my sister Joy. They had a big back garden and an even bigger front yard. Of the two boys, Kamar had the bigger room so he had to give his room to us and stay in his brother's room. Just like at Aunty Karen's house, my mother and her two daughters stayed in one room. The house seemed congested with five children and three adults. For example, we didn't have enough sofa space for everyone to sit on, so the last children to enter the living room usually had to sit on the floor – same thing at dinner time. Also, it seemed someone was always in the bathroom when I wanted to use it, so I always had to wait for my turn.

In the daytime, I spent most of the time playing with the boys outside in the front and back yards. We played ball games, ring games and games that required us to chase the other person until we caught them, then they would have to fulfil our commands.

With our parents' permission, I was allowed to wander off with Kamar and Omar to the nearby sugar cane field where we ate as much sugar cane as our hearts desired. The journey was less than a 5-minute walk. Along the way, everyone we passed would ask Kamar "How is your madda and faada?" Then they would enquire about me asking, "Ah who she?"

I'd often see local people from the area come to the house to chit chat with Aunty Kim when she wasn't at work. Within the first month of staying there, I became aware of all the familiar faces that came to the house or that greeted us on the street - including Uncle Benny, an old man who lived down the road. I don't know how old Uncle Benny was at the time, but I used to hear Aunty Kim say he looked very young for his age; there was hardly any grey hair to be found on his full head of hair. I didn't see him with any walking stick, and he seemed to get on quite independently. Every night he would go to the local shop to drink rum and play dominoes; I knew this because he would talk about his winnings and losses when he came to the house.

After living at Aunty Kim's for about two months, one afternoon I fell asleep and when I woke up, there were no adults in the house. It must have been around 6 or 7pm as it was just starting to get dark outside. I remember feeling hungry and thinking to myself "I'm sure they've not gone too far." I don't remember asking Kamar where our mums were; all I remember was going to look for them. I went to the front yard, but I didn't see anyone. I thought "They must be at Miss Becky's shop, or maybe they're on their way back home." After waiting a few more minutes at the gate, I didn't see any of them coming, so I decided to walk down the road to see if I could see them, or someone else who might be able to tell me where they were. I met up with Uncle Benny a few doors down the road from our house.

He asked me, "what yuh doing on di road by yuhself at this time a night?"

I told him, "Mi ah luk fi mi madda, yuh si har?"

He said, "no, but why you nuh come off di road and I'll luk afta yuh until yuh madda get back?"

I knew I wasn't supposed to talk to strangers, but he wasn't a stranger, he knew my mother and Aunty Kim and they got on very well. At first, I thought I should go back home, but I didn't want to be rude to an elderly friend of the family. I could get in trouble for that, besides, he seemed so nice and caring. Feeling safe, I agreed to go back to his house to wait for my mother there, seeing that it was about a two-minute walk from where we were. Approaching his house, it looked small from the outside but was even smaller inside. There was a small double bed in the right-hand corner of his room, with a sofa chair and a small fridge. The room was dark and had very little space to move around. He asked if I wanted something to eat and I said yes. He offered me bulla and cheese and I gladly accepted it with some milk to wash it down.

After I finished eating, he told me to "lay down and rest yuhself until yuh madda get back. Mi soon guh check fi si if she's der fi yuh."

Somehow, I must have felt so relaxed and ended up falling asleep again. I was awakened by the feeling of my knickers slowly coming down my thighs. I noticed someone was in the bed with me. I froze! It took a few seconds to process where I was. I had so many thoughts rushing through my mind, yet I felt physically paralyzed! Many thoughts and questions went around in my head like "Who's that? What is he doing? Where's my mother? Get up and get out!" I was so scared. I wanted to turn around and scream at whoever it was to stop what they were doing but I couldn't move, not even an inch.

Thinking I was still asleep, the person continued to slowly pull down my knickers. I felt something trying to push between my legs. I couldn't bear it. A thought entered my mind to pretend I'm stretching in my sleep and maybe that will scare the person away. So, I yawned and turned from laying on my side to laying on my back with my eyes closed. I felt the hands pull away quickly and stop touching me. "Yes!" I thought. "It worked!" I wanted to get up and run in case it started again but I was still scared to open my eyes and face that person.

I figured out it must be Uncle Benny, and I didn't want him to know that I knew what he was doing; that may upset him, and I could get into serious trouble for these kinds of accusations. I had to lay there thinking of my next move carefully. I even thought to myself that maybe he had a reasonable explanation for what he was doing; I certainly didn't want to jump to conclusions and hurt his feelings, especially after he had been so nice to me.

Still lying on my back, frightened and scared, another thought came to me that I should slowly get up and do a bigger yawn as if I had just woken up. I did it and found myself sitting up on the bed rubbing my eyes as if to wipe away the sleep. I then turned around to face the person in the bed and my fears were confirmed when I saw Uncle Benny lying beside me. I couldn't believe he would do such a thing! So many thoughts came rushing through my head, but my main priority was to get out, without alarming him.

I asked him, "did my madda cum back?"

He said, "come mek mi tek yuh back to yuh yard and si if she's der."

I was so relieved to hear that, and even more relieved that I didn't seemed to have alarmed him one bit. When I got off the bed, I had to pull my knickers back up, but I did it so quickly without saying a word and was out the door, waiting for him. We walked silently back to where I was staying. Although the walk was less than 5 minutes it seemed much longer.

When I got home, I was so glad to see my mother. She looked upset and worried. I explained briefly that I was at Uncle Benny's house and he gave me something to eat while I was waiting for her to come back home. She thanked Uncle Benny and told me to get in the house. She followed behind me and instructed me to the back garden. As I walked through the house to get to the back garden, it crossed my mind that I may be in trouble for leaving the house without telling anyone where I was going, which must have had my mother worried. But I could never had expected what followed.

My mother questioned me persistently about why I left the house, where I was and what I was doing? I thought I'd already answered these questions, but she still kept asking me, "Who give yuh permission to leave and go to Uncle Benny's yard?" I didn't know if she was asking these questions for her own satisfaction, or maybe she'd picked up on something I was involuntary displaying to her. I remember the angry look on her face and the way her eyes opened up wide – her anger was all over her face. Her tone had changed from her normal voice, but she wasn't shouting as loud as I knew she could. Maybe she was controlling her tone so people in the neighbourhood couldn't hear and find out.

Although I didn't initially intend to tell anyone what had happened, my mother's line of questioning was scaring me, and from past experience I knew not to lie to her, especially if she was already on to me. I thought that by telling the truth she would be mad at Uncle Benny, not me, and rightly so after what he was trying to do to a little child in his room. But instead, my mother got even more angry at me after I told her I fell asleep and woke up to Uncle Benny pulling down my panties and putting something between my legs. She slapped me up in my head with her hands, called me names and accused me of intentionally going to Uncle Benny's yard because I "***wanted man already***."

What's worse is that she threatened me saying, "If yuh ever let anada man touch yuh, luk how mi ah guh do to yuh what Angie did to Tracey."

It was terrifying just remembering what Tracey went through, more-over to think that I may be subjected to the same treatment. Looking back now, I know my mother was just trying to protect me but at the time, I remember feeling so much hurt and injustice!

First of all, no one deserved what Tracey's mother did to her. Secondly, as far as we knew, Tracey voluntarily disobeyed her mother and went to meet her boyfriend whereas I didn't ask for what had happened to me. It was uninvited! I was tricked by Uncle Benny. I didn't do anything wrong, yet I was getting the full punishment. I was confused over the way my mother handled the situation which made me start to feel some resentment towards her. I also began to feel like I couldn't trust to tell her anything else.

The Monster

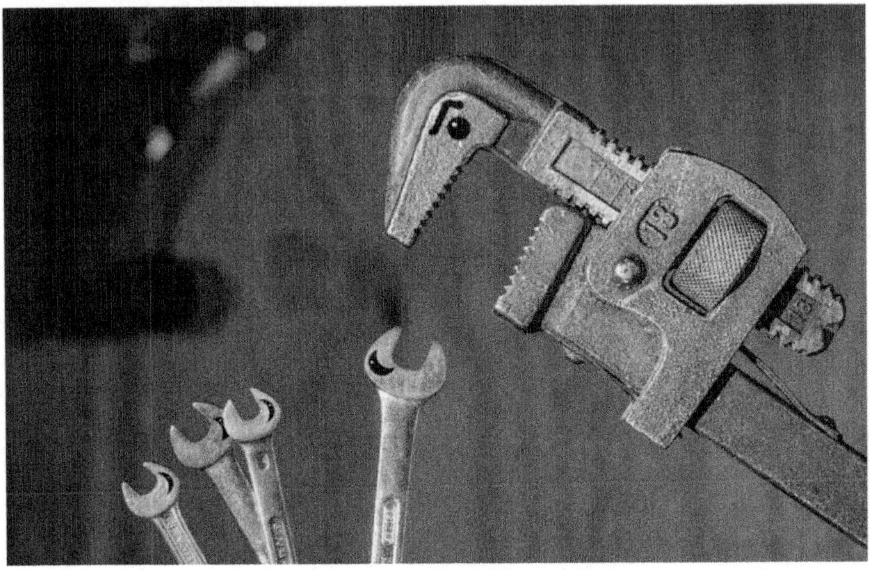

“Domestic abuse is “an incident or pattern of incidents of controlling, coercive, threatening, degrading and violent behaviour, including sexual violence, in the majority of cases by a partner or ex-partner, but also by a family member or carer. It is very common. In the vast majority of cases it is experienced by women and is perpetrated by men.” [5]

“Domestic abuse affects 1 in 4 women... leading to, on average, two women being murdered each weeks due to a current or former partner” [6]

After the situation with Uncle Benny, my next key recollection is standing at a crossroads with my mother, attempting to escape

5 https://www.womensaid.org.uk/information-support/what-is-domestic-abuse/

6 http://www.lwa.org.uk/understanding-abuse/statistics.htm incident occurred.

domestic violence from my step-dad, not knowing what to expect next. But how did we get there?

I don't remember how long we stayed at Aunty Kim's house after ***the incident***, but I do remember celebrating my 6th birthday there. I didn't have a big party, just a small cake with candles while the children in the house sang happy birthday to me. I felt a little special, though not the same since ***the incident occurred***.

When I looked at my mother's face, she smiled at me, yet behind the smiles, all I saw was sadness and worry – something I wished I could change but knew I couldn't – so I blamed myself for the added burden I'd caused on her. The forbidden act of talking about ***the incident*** meant I could never say to her what I really wanted to, and so an invisible glass barrier developed between my mother and I which still exists to this very day.

Within a year after my birthday, we moved to Mount Airy in Negril to live with Joy's dad. His name was Ken and he was a local farmer and professional chef, working at the Rick's Café - one of the most famous tourist restaurants in Negril. Ken was very tall, dark and muscular with a full beard around his face and thick black afro, excluding the few grey hairs at the front of his head. He always had an afro-pick comb in his hair, which he often used to comb his hair backwards as if it was some sort of fashion. His arms were thick and muscular, though one of his hands was disfigured from a previous work accident in a kitchen. However, this didn't seem to stop or limit what he could or couldn't do with both hands. He was wellknown in his community, and I often heard stories about how he fought off 7 police officers at the same time. He almost seemed like a god, and I wished my dad was just like him – strong, courageous and responsible! The only thing I questioned was that he seemed much older than my mother, because his eldest children looked the same age or even older than her, and somehow that didn't feel right. My mother was in her twenties and he must have been in his forties, but if they were happy, then so be it.

We lived in a small boarded house within a massive yard with many other houses, a night club owned by Uncle P, and a small shop owned by Miss Bee. I came to understand this was a family land so everyone who lived here were all related, although Ken seemed to be more of a distant relative than the others. Across the road were many other houses. Directly in front of our house was a huge house with a massive mango tree; the branches hung over the gate allowing some of the mangoes to fall onto the road or on the pedestrian pathway. I used to sit in my yard, looking out for mangoes as they fall off the trees and I'd run to pick them up from the roadside before anything or anyone else get them. Mangoes were my favorite fruit, and these ones were so delicious!

Most of our neighbors were very friendly, especially Miss Bee and Uncle P; they were brothers and sisters to the other two homeowners on the land, Miss Bev and Uncle Bobby. The four brothers and sisters lived in their own homes with their children but overall, they all seemed to live good on the land, especially seeing their children playing together, or when they had family get-togethers. It reminded me of my own family setting in Salt Spring, Montego Bay which is where I've always felt I truly belonged. Being so conscious of this made me felt like I didn't fit into their environment, nevertheless I was glad we finally had our own home instead of sharing other people's.

Things changed quickly that confused me even more. On one hand, Ken seemed to have informally adopted me and treated me almost the same as his own daughter, Joy. He would buy us the same clothes, talk to us and discipline us the same. No matter how hard I searched for it, I couldn't find any major differences in how Joy and I were treated at home. This meant a great deal to me for two reasons: firstly, I knew I wasn't his daughter and so he had no obligations to treat me like one.

Secondly, I had no idea where my biological father was, and I knew he wasn't looking after me like Ken was. Wanting to fit in and belong, as well as my admiration for Ken made everything seem perfect for him to adopt me – and so, I chose to call him "daddy" to show him the love and respect I felt he deserved.

But on the other hand, Ken started to beat my mother badly and often. One punch in her face and her little body would fly to the ground. Her black eye would last at least a week and it broke my heart to see her in that condition. I thought of him as an evil monster for doing that to my mother. I had never seen anyone hit my mother before. In fact, I'd never seen any adult hit another so badly, especially someone they say they care about and love. I never knew what my mother could've done to deserve it, and I couldn't understand how he could treat her that way or why she put up with it. I thought that it was simple, if he loved her, treat her well and if he didn't love her, then let her go.

Caught between the love-hate relationship with Ken, I wanted more than anything for him to stop beating my mother, so I didn't care if it meant losing him as a father; my mother was the only consistent person in my life up to that point, and I loved her no matter what.

However, the good times with Ken soon came around again such as Easter and Christmas, and everything would seem so perfect again. Ken and my mother would seem so happy and loving on these occasions, which would make me think he was changing for the better, and that everything would be ok. It was hard to see him as the monster he was when he was being so nice, gentle and happy – until the next time he hits her, and I would feel let down and just want to run away again. It felt like my emotions were constantly on the alert, going up and down, causing me to be vigilant, anxious and distressed.

I didn't realise the extent of his power or control over my mother, or how financially dependent she was on him. Yet I still hated him for how I perceived things to be at the time! I knew I was helpless to do anything about it, and I definitely didn't want to overstep the boundaries or get caught in the firing line of having him or my mother taking out their anger on me. I'd be so relieved when the neighbours tried to intervene such as Uncle P and Miss Bee, but Ken would threaten them with his machete, so they chose not to get involved. Later I'd hear Ken blaming my mother for the neighbours' involvement and I'd hear her screaming. I wished that more people would get involved and save her, but when no one else did. I knew we were on our own. I covered my ears through the screaming, punching and banging, waiting for it to finish – without knowing each time if my mother would survive his beatings, or how battered her face would look if she survived. Ken was also loud and spoke very aggressively with mean and deeply insulting words. I remember my mother saying his verbal abuse was often worse than the physical beatings.

Rejecting James

"Research examining battered women populations in refuges has indicated that the presence of domestic violence increases the likelihood of child maltreatment in the family." [7]

"The incidence of child abuse is higher in families with an identified domestic violence problem." [8]

Then came my big brother James, who had been staying with my Aunt Patsy (my mother's half-sister on her mother's side) in Salt Spring. Now that my mother had a "stable" home, she'd brought James to live with us. However, Ken made it clear that James could visit but wasn't allowed to stay. I was heart-broken again. I hadn't seen my brother in years, and just wanted him with us. I thought

7 Giles-Sims 1985; Hughes 1988; Jouriles & Norwood 1995

8 https://aifs.gov.au/cfca/publications/exploring-family-violence-linksbetween-child-maltreatment

I'd feel safer with him around, not that he could do anything about Ken beating our mother, but at least I wouldn't feel so alone. To make things easier, Aunty Patsy moved close to us so James could visit more often. This was okay with Ken but only for a short period. I noticed the more James visited, the more arguments and fighting happened at home.

Things got so bad that James was no longer allowed to visit us. So, my mother secretly arranged with Aunt Patsy for James to visit us when Ken was out at the farm or somewhere else. But one day whilst James was on one of his secret visits at our house, my mother told James to let her know when he could see Ken coming from a distance, up the hill. That morning James spent most of his time in the front yard on the look-out for Ken. Apparently, he stood there until Ken was right next to him in the front yard.

When Ken asked James "wah yuh ah duh yah?" James replied "mummy seh mi fi luk out fi yuh." This made Ken very angry and he stormed into the house and gave my mother a proper beating. I sat in the front yard listening to all the screams and shouting but helpless to do anything to stop it. I thought he was going to kill my mother and nobody would care. I knew he wouldn't get away with it so easily if we were living near my family in Salt Spring. Whilst standing outside pondering over these thoughts, Ken opened the front door and shouted "him betta gone by di time mi come back coz mi nah fatten foul fi mangoose!" I didn't know what "fatten foul fi mangoose" meant but I knew my brother was definitely not welcome in our home, which made me feel so beaten inside.

Shortly after this, Aunt Patsy came to pick up James and took him back to her house. I stayed out of the way until my mother called me in the house to help tidy up. At first, I didn't want to go inside because I didn't know what state my mother's face would be in, and inside the house felt like hell. But I knew that if I let my mum speak to me more than once, I risked facing the wrath of her anger and considering what she'd just been through, there was a lot of anger to release. Although I was losing respect for my mother for putting up with this kind of horrific treatment and for being unable to protect her children from it, I was still very much scared of her, so I felt obliged to do as she said. One look from her sank right through me, and I instantly knew what was to come if I didn't change my behaviour more appropriately or do as she requested.

So, I quickly got up and went to see why she was calling me. She was sitting on the bed in her room folding some clothes that she'd previously washed and dried. I stood near the door where she could see me and when she lifted her head to address me, all I could see was cuts, bruises, blood stains, swollen face and her eyes full of tears. It also looked like her nose had been bleeding as I could see more bloodstains in her nostrils. This shocked me and I froze physically, but my thoughts were going wild. I remember thinking:

"Why am I shocked to see this after everything I've seen before? How could she allow him to do this to her? No one cares about us; we're going to die here if we don't go back to our family in Salt Spring!"

I was angry. I wanted to burst into tears in her arms, but I just stood quietly waiting for her instructions. I was seriously convinced that going back to our home town was the answer to all our problems, and I just couldn't understand why my mother couldn't see that as well.

With all these thoughts going through my mind, I didn't hear my mother when she instructed me to go to the shop to buy her some Panadol painkillers, rubbing alcohol, bread and eggs. She didn't give me any money to buy these as she had an existing tab at our local shop, which Ken usually settled at the end of each week. All I saw were her lips moving but I was still deep in my own thoughts and couldn't process anything she was saying. Her lips finished moving; she was looking at me and I was still staring at her. I didn't know what to do. In a caring tone, I said "mummy yuh alright?" She just nodded her head and repeated her instructions in a calmer voice than I ever expected. I quickly went to the shop and back. I could tell by the shameful looks on the faces of everyone I passed on the way, that they knew what had just happened at our house. I ignored them and hastily returned home without anyone saying anything to me. By the time I got back, mum was cooking dinner like nothing had ever happened. This played on my mind for the rest of the night as I couldn't believe what my life was like and there was nothing, I could do about it. The best I could hope for, was to keep out of the way so I didn't do anything to get into trouble, as that would make me feel even worse.

At the Crossroads

"On average, women stay in an abusive relationship for 2.6 years before they leave. Both remaining in an abusive relationship and leaving it can bring risks of harm and benefits to the women themselves, their children, family members and friends. Leaving can be a particularly dangerous time for women and children, as partners begin to lose some of the control they previously had and may retaliate. Similarly, staying can be dangerous as the risk of further abuse is likely to escalate as partners increasingly feel they can get away with it." [9]

A few days after the latest incident, I was in the front yard playing. My mother was sitting on the huge rock stone that lay at the side of the house where she was hand-washing some clothes. She used a blue solid bar of soap commonly known as 'cake-soap' that usually

9 https://healthtalk.org/womens-experiences-domestic-violence-and-abuse/womens-coping-strategies-for-domestic-violence-and-abuse

made the clothes smell so fresh and the whites look whiter. When the soap water splashed on her legs and feet it left white marks that made it look as if her legs hadn't been moisturised in years.

I can remember the familiar loud sound that came from her firm grip of the clothes and rubbing them together. Back then in Jamaica, if you were hand-washing clothes and it didn't make a similar sound, it seemed like you weren't doing it properly, which is funny because not everyone knew how to make that sound with their hands, yet many of them still washed perfectly clean clothes.

Still playing in the front yard, I suddenly noticed that 'clothes washing sound' had stopped and I heard my mother's footsteps coming towards me. I could never have expected what she was about to say. In a low but anxious voice she looked at me and said, "Come on, we leaving!" She was still bare-footed and looked tired and dirty but I didn't care. I had longed to hear those words so badly that I instantly stopped what I was doing, jumped up from the ground, and gave her my full attention, ready to follow her lead. It felt like Christmas, Easter and my birthday all in that one moment.

She took my right hand and we started walking. Without any bags or change of clothes, we walked out of the yard on the road and continued walking towards the main town in Negril. I don't recall anyone saying anything to us along the way. We walked silently for about 20 minutes then we came to a crossroads and stopped. My heart leapt because I didn't want to stop. Initially I thought this was too good to be true, but the more we walked the more I was starting to believe that we were finally ending that horrific part of our lives. Somehow, as we stopped, I instantly knew we weren't going any further. Still holding my mother's hand, I looked up at her and saw her looking to the left and then to the right. She kept doing this as if she was confused and not sure where to go next. After a few seconds passed, she turned to face me. My heart was racing. I didn't want to hear what she had to say; I was too scared to have my thoughts confirmed. My heart ached as she finally said the words so casually,

"Oh mi nuh no wha mi ah do. We cya leave without no clothes or money. We affi guh back fi get money and then wi cyan leave."

It's like she'd come to her senses and was thinking more rationally, but I knew we were never going to leave again anytime soon. The little hope I'd regained in those few moments of attempting to escape had instantly vanished, leaving me with nothing but despair! It was so unfair. It didn't matter to me which way we'd turn, left or right. It didn't matter if we had to sleep on the streets for a while; I was more than ready to end that part of my life by any means necessary.

We walked back to the house in silence but the way I was feeling inside was completely different. In a matter of minutes, I went from feeling over-excited and hopeful to feelings of despair, disappointment and anger. My mother became my enemy in my mind. I saw her as the person bringing me back into that painful environment that she couldn't protect me from. I thought she was so weak; she couldn't even see my pain. I blamed her for the hurt and disappointment I was feeling inside. If she couldn't do it for herself, she could've done it for me, I thought. Maybe she loved Ken so much – even more than her children – that she couldn't bring herself to leave him. Or maybe she was too scared to leave him. Either way, I thought she was too weak and of no use to me. I knew I couldn't rely on her to protect or keep me safe. She couldn't even protect her own self! I wanted to scream so badly but I couldn't allow myself to show her that amount of vulnerability and weakness in me. So I firmed it until we got back to the house; I found a quiet place and cried silently to myself. I hated my life and there was no hope to change it. The more I thought about it, the more painful it felt and I knew we were never going to try escaping again anytime soon, definitely not that day. About an hour after we got back, my mother came to make sure I wouldn't say anything to anyone, especially Ken, about our attempted escape, and promised me that we will try again soon. Needless to say, that day didn't come around anytime soon.

My emotions were so overwhelming that I didn't stop for a moment to think about what my mother was going through; the deep-rooted fear, guilt and responsibility she must have been feeling because of her unsuccessful attempt at trying to escape domestic violence with her children; how she'd risked her life to escape without any money, support or a 'Safety Plan'. What would've happened to her or her children if Ken had found out? Although I didn't think about it at the time, I noticed many changes in her after that day which affected her strength, self-esteem, confidence and her general character from the person I'd known her to be. We've never really spoken about it just like all the other things that had happen before and after this day. Looking back now, I can imagine how frightened yet defeated she must have felt, and the immense strength it must have taken for her to have tried escaping the violence and control. I now appreciate this attempted escape a million-fold. I appreciate her courage, strength and willpower. But the odds seemingly were against her: no women why - like many other female victims - she returned back to her extremely violent perpetrator!

According to the UK's National Domestic Violence Hotline, women victims usually make several attempts to leave, before making the final break. [10] It is not to be undermined how extremely difficult this first attempted escape was for my mother and her children. I wish there had been organizations at the time in Jamaica that could've helped make her attempt successful by offering her

10 https://www.nationaldahelpline.org.uk

emotional and practical support, such as making an appropriate Safety Plan. Sitting here with these thoughts, I can't help but to wonder selfishly if my mother had the right support at the time, how different my life may have been.

Heskit Life

"Witnessing domestic abuse is really distressing and scary for a child, and causes serious harm. Children living in a home where domestic abuse is happening are at risk of other types of abuse too." [11]

"Almost a million children in Britain are affected by domestic violence, either as victims or witnesses." [12]

---

11 https://www.nspcc.org.uk/preventing-abuse/child-abuse-and-neglect/ domestic-abuse/

12 https://www.independent.co.uk/news/uk/crime/domestic-violence-affects-one-million-children-in-the-uk-7584593.html

We continued living in the same house for about another year whilst Ken was building a new home further away from the main road and everyone we knew. This was a more secluded part of the area called Heskit, about 10 minutes-drive from the main road, where we lived. Although we were closer to the local primary and secondary school called Mount Airy All Age School, there were hardly any street lights. Many homes including ours couldn't afford electricity. We either had to steal it or do without by using candles or kerosene oil lamps. There were extreme water shortages, patchy and unfinished roads with deep potholes. Some taxi drivers refused to drive on this road and instead would leave you on the main road for you to make your own way to Heskit, with or without any luggage. We also had to walk past many tall trees, thick bushes and a cemetery which was the scariest thing to do alone at nights.

Our new home was similar to the house we were living in before, but we had much more free outdoor space, as we didn't have to share with anyone anymore. There were bushes and tall trees surrounding the house including fruit trees such as mangoes, tamarind and ackee trees. I got excited thinking of the adventures I was going to have exploring the area. Ken used a large part of the land for his farming and raising animals such as goats, pigs, chickens and a few cows. He planted all kinds of food including bananas, potatoes, corn, yam, pumpkin etc. He sold crops to neighbours to raise income, and the animals he often killed were sold in pieces, although some were sold whole as they were.

Every Sunday morning, Ken would butcher an animal, mainly a goat, depending on demand and needs. He'd march the goat from the farm into our front yard, then tie it upside down on the strong ackee tree and leave it for a few minutes. After waiting for its blood to drain into its head, he'd slit its throat. He'd then wait for the blood to finish draining from the carcass's body into the ground, before removing the animal's skin with a knife and his bare hands. He'd cut the legs and head from the rest of its body, cut open its belly, remove the tripe and put it in the big pots for cleaning - usually done by myself or another sibling. He usually gave my mother the liver and/or kidney to prepare for breakfast and some of the meat for dinner. The rest of the animal parts, including its belly, tripe, head and legs were sold to various people in the community. I used to enjoy burning and scraping the hair off the head and feet over wood fire. Sometimes my mother or Ken would use the goat's head and feet to make manish water (a form of Caribbean soup) which was my favourite, alongside curry goat with rice and peas. I also used to enjoy roasting the ram goat's seed (cock) and eating it. Sometimes we'd even fight over it. I cringed writing this! I'm now aware these were slavery food. It sounds so disgusting to think I not only ate but really enjoyed it. Is this what guilty pleasure is? I thought about omitting this bit from my book but chose not to, as this lifestyle was a normal part of my reality at the time.

Our house consisted of two bedrooms only. My mother and Ken shared one room and I shared the other room with Joy. There was no separate living or dining space and no indoor toilet or kitchen. We went to toilet in the bushes during the day whilst at nights, we used a potty (otherwise known as chimney) in the house. Joy was always the person responsible for emptying and washing the household chimney in the morning before she went to school, but she didn't always remember and often got into trouble for leaving the used chimney in the house all day. Many times, she wouldn't remember the chimney until the night when someone asked to use it. From that look in her eyes, I can only imagine how shocked and nervous she instantly felt upon realizing she hadn't taken out or washed the chimney again!

We cooked on wood fire and washed our dishes at the back of the house using two containers of water - one for washing and the other for rinsing. I used to love seeing those big black pots cooking on the wood fire, which gave the food a bit of a "smoked flavour", and made it taste even more delicious. As we didn't have a microwave, oven or cooker, it meant we had to cook and warm up everything on the wood fire, even in the rain. We never ran out of wood as there were so many bushes and trees around us. I do miss the smoked flavour in my food and the slightly burnt bits at the bottom of the pot - we called it 'bun bun' or 'pot bottom'. Over the years my siblings and I would fight over washing the pots so we could get the bun bun, haha! Aww the good 'ole days and the simple treasures of life. Most children of today would never understand this, seeing as it's to do with chores and completely unrelated to electronic devices or the internet.

Ken was a professional chef and he taught my mother how to cook, properly. Between the two of them, our meals were always tasty no matter what was on the menu. They used to cook excess food in large pots, so the food could be rationed and last a few days. As I wasn't a picky child when it came to my food, I'd always be looking forward to my next meal, even if was the same thing we'd had for the past few days. Joy on the other hand didn't eat much. I used to hurry up and finish my food, waiting for Joy to say she didn't want hers, so I could quickly ask my mother if I could have it. Sometimes mother would say "yes, nyam it." Other times she'd say "no, you wah drop boof and mek she drop ping?!"

Living in Heskit was strange at first. Although it was a community neighbourhood where everyone knew everyone, I didn't know anyone there. I came to understand that the people who lived there were all Ken's family. I felt stuck, as Ken's scary side really freaked me out, and based on his reputation, I knew that no-one could challenge him or save us, even if they wanted to. I told myself there's a positive side to this situation; we were untouchable! No one would dare mess with us as they'd have Ken to deal with.

I was about 7 years old and I still called Ken daddy. I still had mixed emotions about him. I was deeply grateful to him for treating me the same as his own daughter, Joy. I'd come to realize that a child as brown-skinned as Joy would generally be more favourable over a darker skinned child like myself. My mother and Ken bought Joy and I the same clothes and always dressed us like twins. I respected him for that and held him in high regard. But I couldn't get my head around the ferocious way he treated my mother, or the violent way he'd discipline Joy and I, like he was fighting an enemy on the road. When things were bad, they were really bad. When things were good, we knew not to get too comfortable in case anyone of us did something to piss him off.

At home no-one seemed to care about my scars, both internally from all the hurt and pain and externally, from really harsh beatings. I had to find a way to cope and be happy with the life I had. I found comfort in my education when I started to go to school. It became an escape mechanism for me to physically be away from the house, as well as providing me hope for my future.

Ken continued to beat my mother as and when he felt like it. I used to hear my mother say that if a week passed by and there weren't any problems in the house, she'd be on edge in anticipation of what's coming next. One night, Ken hit my mother so hard she fell on the bed and didn't move. Thinking our mum was dead, Joy and I panicked, grabbed a frying pan and started hitting Ken with it. We were very scared about what he would do to us, but for that split second, we didn't care until he grabbed the frying pan from us and we both ran into our room and hid under the bed – we were terrified!

Was our mother ok? Was Ken coming after us? We must have fallen asleep underneath the bed praying he don't come into our room. We were awakened the following morning by the sound of my mother's voice, calling out to get up, as if nothing had happened the night before. For some strange reason this brought comfort to me, hearing my mother calling my name in her usual way. Joy and I were both thankful to still be alive as well as knowing that our mother was ok too. Although no-one ever spoke about what had happened that night, Joy and I were on high alert thinking Ken could say or do something to us at any time.

The more my mother was being violently abused, the more anger she took out on us when she was disciplining us. At times she would use anything that came to hand to hit me. From a shoe with/without heels, to a thick piece of stick with sharp edges to thick belts that broke on my skin. I got the most beats in the house, especially as I had started to steal and tell lies. However, we all lived in a warzone in that house.

The Beginning

"A child is sexually abused when they are forced or persuaded to take part in sexual activities. This doesn't have to be a physical contact and it can happen online. Sometimes the child won't understand that what's happening to them is abuse. They may not even understand that it's wrong. Or they may be afraid to speak out." [13]

When I was around 8 years old, my mother fell pregnant with her third child with Ken. They both seemed happy about the pregnancy and I'd hope that it would make things get better. My mother was working during her pregnancy as she'd set up a small stall at my school selling snacks and drinks to the school children during break and lunch time. As the school was only a stone's throw away from our house, it made it easier for my mother to go back

13 https://www.nspcc.org.uk/what-is-child-abuse/types-of-abuse/child-sexualabuse/

and forth. Sometimes after school, my mother had to go into town to replace her stocks and buy groceries for the house. Usually when she left us in the house, there would be very strict instructions not to leave the yard and often chores were delegated to be completed before her return.

One day when my mother was out, no chores were given, just simple instructions not to leave the yard. Joy and I were in the front yard playing when I heard Ken shouted my name. The way he called me made me quickly jumped up, leave what I was doing and ran to him out of fear I'd done something wrong, or hadn't done something I was supposed to. It felt very familiar; like I was in big trouble and knew what to expect, but still dreaded it! I followed his voice and found him in his room. I was used to getting myself into trouble without even realizing it, so I waited anxiously for him to speak. He instructed me to close the door behind me and sit on his bed. It felt strange, but I didn't question it. He started asking me questions that made me even more uncomfortable, confused and embarrassed:

"Yuh have ah boyfriend?"

I said "No", wondering who's been telling lies on me now?!

"Anybody eva touch yuh dere?" he asked, pointing to my private part.

My body froze for a few seconds. I was confused! I was still wondering whether I was in trouble, and if this had something to do with it. I expected him to be angry, but his tone and body language was saying something completely different. I couldn't figure out fast enough what was happening. This scared me even more, because I couldn't stop it or prepare myself for it – I didn't even know what 'IT' was!

Conscious of how my delayed response could anger him, with a slightly embarrassed yet scared look on my face, I answered "No".

"Yuh no wat dis is?" he asked as he held my right hand and put it inside the zip-hole of his trousers – which was already down – to touch his penis.

I couldn't believe what was happening! I thought I was having a seriously bad dream and wanted to wake from it, but I couldn't. I was so nervous, my heart pumped loudly in my chest. To this day I can still remember holding this huge, warm and hard thing in my hand, that had a lot of thick hair around it. IT felt so weird! I didn't know what to do.

The situation reminded me of Uncle Benny poking me from behind with something I imagine looked the same, the only difference is now I'm holding it with much disgust in my hand. All those feelings I'd buried came rushing back, but this time my level of discomfort and confusion was at maximum capacity. I didn't have time to process any of what was going on; I just tried to remain calm and attentive so as not to upset him or hurt his feelings, as I was sure that would land me in more trouble. I don't think he realized I didn't verbally answer his question, but as I found myself moving my hand slowly on his penis, he must've taken that as my response. I didn't know what I was doing but judging by the look on his face, he seemed to like it.

After a few minutes, he made me stop and took my panties off. I didn't know what was going on or what to expect. I just did as he said. Although he was acting normal like everything was fine, it felt so wrong! I think I was still in deep shock; I was just doing as I was told without thinking too much about it. He laid on top of me, using his "half good" left hand to balance his weight on the bed so he wouldn't compress me with his full weight. I could hardly breathe laying under him. He started kissing me, more like sucking on my lips, really hard. I hated it. I hated the rough hair on his face which rubbed against mine and went into my mouth. He sucked on my lips so hard that they were burning – I thought they'd fall off!

He then used the very fat and thick fingers of his right hand – the good hand – to caress inside and out of my vagina. It felt strange, but nice. I couldn't understand what he was doing to me or why it felt somewhat pleasing to me. More scary thoughts came rushing through my mind which I blocked out in order to continue giving him my attention.

He used his right hand to hold his penis and brought it up to my private area, then started to push it against the opening of my vagina. I felt instant pain as he did this. I stopped myself from screaming out loud but still gave a little "arghhh" sound. I remember him staring at me, observing how much pain I could bear before he'd pull away and try again. One of the main issues with this process is that I was hiding a lot more of the pain than I was letting on. I so wanted him to realize this and stop, but he didn't. "Doesn't he care about me anymore?" I lay there wondering to myself.

He tried to force his penis more and more into my vagina until it couldn't go any further. The more he did this the harder his penis became, and the faster he continued until he suddenly jumped off me and held his penis in his hands!

He sat up on the bed, leaning forward silently with his head held down in front of him. I couldn't see what he was doing as his back was turned to me. I didn't know why he got up so suddenly or what he was doing with his penis. I didn't know what to do. Was he coming back? If not, did I do something wrong? Was he upset with me, or had he suddenly realized what he was doing was wrong? Should I keep laying down or get up and put my panties (knickers) back on?

With all these thoughts rushing through my mind, I kept still on the bed waiting for further instructions. After a couple of minutes, he stood up with tissue in his hand, covering his penis. He pulled on his trousers and said to me, "Yuh cyan gwan back outside but don't yuh eva seh ah word to anybody!" I got up, put my panties back on and went back outside without even checking to see what state I was in down there.

The End?

"A suicide attempt is an attempt where a person tries to commit suicide but survives." [14]

"A person who seriously wishes to end their own suffering can also fail in their attempt. This 'failure' could be due to ignorance, lack of knowledge about what is required, what to do and what to expect." [15]

"Suicide attempts usually come from a place of despair, hopelessness and worthlessness." [16]

14 https://en.wikipedia.org/wiki/Suicide_attempt

15 http://seize-today.tripod.com/anintroductiontosuicide/id6.html

16 https://centerfordiscovery.com/difference-self-harm-attempted-suicide/

I knew I couldn't go back to playing with Joy. I wasn't the same child she was playing with a few moments ago. Everything had changed, and I didn't want to pretend otherwise. Besides, I was overwhelmed with so many thoughts and emotions rushing through me. I remember feeling completely deflated, confused, punished, dirty, embarrassed and scared. I genuinely didn't know who this monster was anymore. As bad as he was, I thought I knew him. I knew what to expect from him generally whether good or bad. I called him 'daddy' because I thought he was a better man than my own father. One thing for sure now though, he definitely wasn't my father because my father would never do that to me! I hated him!! A thought crossed my mind to tell someone. But who would believe me? And even if they did, who would be brave enough to confront him? I was completely broken and hopeless. It felt like all life had left my body except my mind, which was automatically functioning against my will and seemingly, out of my control. More and more thoughts flooded my mind. I just wanted it to stop. I started to run, cry and scream "NOOOO!" I didn't even care if anyone saw or heard me.

My mind was racing out of control, and in a desperate plight to make sense of it all, I started to analyze and compare Ken to Uncle Benny. "What Ken did was so much worse," I thought. "He went all the way staring right in my eyes!" I couldn't get his face out of my head, nor his hair out of my mouth, nor his lips off mine, nor the touch of his penis off my hands.

How could he do this to me? I felt violated and it was all his fault! What did I do to deserve this?! I thought he loved me as his daughter - I thought I ***was*** his daughter! I was so confused. It buried what was left of me into the ground, thinking that he did it to me ***because*** I wasn't his daughter. I hated him even more – much more than I could possibly hate anyone else.

I don't know when I stopped running but I found myself walking at a fast pace, not knowing where to go. I couldn't go back home to see him or face what he'd done. I couldn't control the thoughts pouring through my mind causing a warzone, or the headache or chest pain. I saw a tall tree in front of me and something made me climb it. Next thing I knew I was hanging off a branch with one hand looking down. I believed that jumping off that tree would solve everything; or at least put an end to my pain and suffering. I felt hopeless, useless, worthless and completely damaged. I thought there was no coming back. My life was over and there was no point in trying to fight it.

Without thinking any further, I let go – but I landed with my feet firmly on the ground. I was so shocked and disappointed that it didn't work. Instead, I felt even more useless, and still had those overwhelming feelings rushing through me. I had to try again. This time I tried to force myself not to land on my feet again. I attempted it once more, telling myself over and over not to land on my feet – but the same thing happened. This made me even more upset. I dropped to the ground and cried and cried and cried!

I felt like my pain was endless and impossible to get away from. I couldn't bear it anymore, and yet I couldn't escape it either. I felt forced to accept it. I told myself not to feel anything at all. Block it out and pretend it didn't happen. Whilst I was in the bushes trying to console myself, I heard my mother shouting for me. I slowly started walking towards her, not caring how long it took or if I'd be in trouble once I got there. I just didn't care anymore because for the first time I thought, "What's the worst that can happen?!"

My mother had just returned from the market/supermarket and needed help unpacking the shopping. I did as I was told but without any enthusiasm. I was still trying to control the thoughts and emotions my body was naturally producing, however in my mind, I started to blame my mother. I blamed her for moving us here, for the horrific treatments we'd suffered, and for living with this monster who had just done something really terrible to me, and now I can't even tell anyone. All I could think of was that day at the crossroads; "If only my mother had the necessary courage to escape, this would never have happened!" I lost a lot of respect for my mother that day. But she didn't seem to notice anything different as she never said anything to me, which made me feel even more hopeless.

We carried on living as "normal" and my mother soon had her baby which turned out to be a girl. There was no drama in our home for a few months. But I was never the same child since that day in the room with Ken. I made a promise to myself not to call him daddy anymore, because I was convinced that he didn't see me as his daughter, otherwise he couldn't have done that to me. It crossed my mind whether he had or would do the same thing to Joy, so I was vigilantly watching over Joy, but I didn't see anything to raise my suspicion. On one hand I found comfort in knowing that Joy never had such a horrible experience, but on the other hand, I became even more convinced and angry at the thought that he only did it to me because I wasn't his daughter. It highlighted to me a sense of not being wanted (at least not in the way I thought I should've been). Another thing that changed within me was that I became withdrawn and often stayed in my own company at home. I started getting into fights at school, whilst the beatings at home got worse.

Ken didn't stop at that one time either; he continued to sexually abuse me whenever he got the chance, until it became a regular occurrence. It felt like I was his "bit on the side". The more attempts he made to have sex with me, the more I had to bear the pain to allow him to brace his penis further and further into my vagina.

Over time, I started to develop emotions towards his attention, touches and sexual advances. I hated myself for it, but I couldn't help it. I even started to make myself available to him when I knew my mother wouldn't be around. If more than a month passed and he didn't "call for me", I'd start to get upset and worried that he didn't want me anymore. I got jealous when I saw him publicly displaying affection towards my mother. I even got some pleasure out of seeing him beating her because I knew it would create distance between the two of them which meant more opportunities for Ken and I to spend time together.

My emotions were extremely overwhelming and all over the place. It felt like I had no control whatsoever over myself or my situation. Sometimes I'd get beatings from Ken and didn't know why. I couldn't understand how Ken could beat me so badly one day, then the next he'd be all over me telling me I'm his "special girl".

My fighting at school and home got worse, and this along with telling lies and stealing, made me a scapegoat to my mother's beatings too. Anytime anything happened, as soon as anyone in our home or community mentioned my name, I'd be in big trouble. I don't think certain adults realised the amount of trouble they got me in. In Jamaica, adults are more likely to be believed over children, especially "lying" and "troublesome" children like myself.

On many occasions, I was never given the opportunity to give my side of the story before the beatings began. I'd be left in so much pain, wondering what I ever did to deserve it. It got so bad, I stopped caring and started to rebel; I started doing whatever I wanted because I already knew what would happen. For example, if my mother left us tasks to do with instructions like "do not leave the yard", I'd wait a little while, then walk right through the gate or wonder off into the bushes behind our house, and not come back until shortly before her return. Sometimes she'd return while I was still up in the bushes, and I would suddenly hear her shouting for me. My heart would pound so fast and my stomach would churn in anticipation of what to expect, but that didn't stop me from doing it again the next time.

At 10 years old, my mother had another child for Ken. By this time, they had 4 children together, plus me. They brought my big brother James back to live with us. I suspect the reason for this was so he could help out with the chores and look after the younger ones. I can still hear Ken's resistance to James, "mi nah fatten foul fi mangoose". He never did like James. I thought maybe it was because my brother was a boy and he couldn't get his way in the same way he could with me, or perhaps my brother would try to protect us from him.

I didn't realize just how badly this all affected James's masculinity, self-belief and worthiness. I can see how this still impacts many areas of his adult life. The sad thing is, like many of us, he can't always see it. Even when he does, his emotions become unbearable, causing further barriers for him to actually deal with it effectively. So, he turns a blind eye and focuses his attention on something else, which distracts him from the real pain.

The main things I got into trouble for at this age were wetting my bed, theft, lies and fighting. I hated how the beatings made me feel; hated and rejected, especially because I was never told anything contrary like "I love you." The more mischief I got up to, the scarier "that look" in my mother's eyes became – and the more defiant I got. I remembered when one look from my mother would send chills up my spine and I'd do exactly as she wished, but that was when I thought of her as my mother and when I knew she cared. By this time, I was convinced that she couldn't be my mother. It puzzled me for a long time how my mother could be so firm and serious in disciplining me when she wasn't able to protect me from abuse or violence in our home. She couldn't see the pain and suffering in my eyes, nor could she see that my wrongdoings were a cry for help!

Church

I completely lost hope in my mother and started going to church as a way of escaping the madness at home, both physically and mentally. I went to Good Hope Seventh Day Adventist Church in Negril. I loved the feeling I got from church, just by entering the building and feeling humbled to be in such a holy place. I loved the people with their cheerful smiles, welcoming and caring characters. I felt free, safe, worthy and accepted in the blood of Jesus, especially when I was singing the hymns or listening to the scripture readings. I found meaning for myself in everything that was taking place. Crusades gave an even more vibrant feeling that made me come alive inside, a feeling I thought I'd never experience again. I felt so wonderful and empowered, like I could do anything in those moments. A crusade is a series of religious campaigns held by senior church members to save souls for Christ. The first crusade I attended was held on a beach in Negril Town; I had no idea how the preaching would hit me inside. By the second night I felt an irresistible calling to give my life to Christ, for him to save me from all my troubles. I wanted it so badly that I didn't ask any questions. All that mattered was how it made me ***feel***. I felt connected to something good and more powerful than myself. For the first time, I felt there was more to my life than what was happening at home. I put my name down immediately to get baptized. When I was dipped in the water and came back up, I thought that all my troubles would be over; as they sang the songs, I rejoiced over my new hopeful path ahead. But it wasn't. It got worse.

Doctor Visit

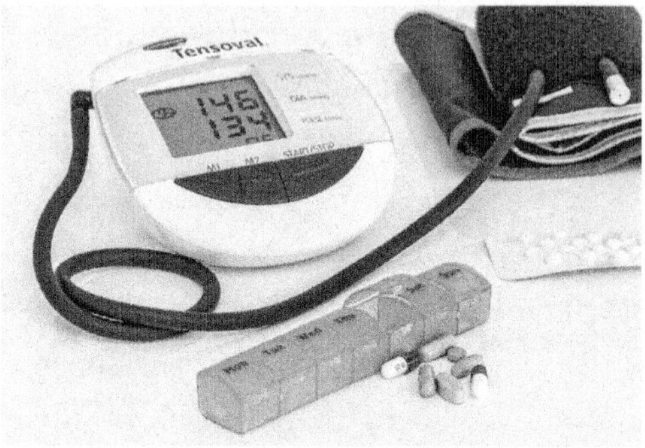

I started to feel sick in my stomach, almost every day. The pain got so bad that I couldn't bear it anymore. I knew I had to tell my mother so she could take me to the doctor, but I was scared – really, really scared. I was scared of telling anyone what I thought was causing the pain. I thought my mother would beat the hell out of me and hate me even more without trying to hide it. I thought the doctors would call the police and lock me up in jail and even worse, I thought that Ken would kill me and my mother. My fears grew with the pain and I was caught in a dark limbo between the excruciating pain, or believing my life would be cut short if I said anything. Then I suddenly thought, "What if I'm pregnant?" This thought brought about even more fears and life-changing thoughts such as "what would people say?" "Would I be allowed to keep my baby?" "What would my baby call my siblings?" I had no idea that I couldn't get pregnant until after I'd started seeing my period. These countless thoughts haunted me, but then one day the pain was so bad that my mother caught me holding my belly and started asking me questions. I told her that I was having really bad tummy pain but didn't say anything else. She asked me if I had started seeing my period and I said no. She gave me Panadol painkillers and told me to rest for a little while. I lay in my bed but the pain didn't ease.

A couple of hours later she came to check on me; seeing I was still in pain, told me that I needed to see the doctor. She instructed my brother James to take me. We had to walk about 30 minutes to get to the main road in order to get a taxi. This was the longest walk of my life. When we got to the doctors, I immediately noticed how close the police station was to the hospital; I could even see it through the doctor's office. I remember it was a male doctor although I can't remember his name. After having to wait another 30 minutes, the doctor told my brother to wait outside so he could examine me. In the examination room, he told me to lay on the bed so he could examine my belly. As he poked around it, I responded with arghh sounds when I felt the pain getting worse. He asked if I could take my trousers and panties (knickers) off so he could get a better check. I did as I was told. He didn't take long examining 'down there' before he told me to get up and put my clothes back on. He said I should return to his office once I'm done, then he left the room. I was so scared with overwhelming thoughts going through my mind and still in pain. I didn't want to go back to his office, but I knew I had to. I slowly went to pee in the toilet and then I knocked on his office door.

My brother opened the door and came out. I was staring at him as if to ask "What are you doing in here?" but the words didn't come out. Instead, I stood there staring even after my brother had closed the door behind him. Then I heard a voice say "Please take a seat." I sat and waited anxiously. The doctor turned to me and asked many questions including: "Do you know why your belly is hurting you? Is anyone hurting you?" He pleaded with me to tell him and promised that he'll ensure I'm protected from any further problems. He said "I can make it stop but you have to tell me the truth." The window right above the doctor's head was open, and I was looking straight at the police station in fear of what the next step would be if I opened my mouth and said anything. I thought the doctor seemed nice, but I was sure he couldn't protect me from my step-dad. After all what I'd seen him do to my mother, and the stories I'd heard about what he'd done to other people – everyone in our neighbourhood was scared of him. I was convinced that if the doctor met him, he'd be scared of him too! I couldn't risk my life and the life of my family for this doctor so I kept quiet. The doctor soon gave up trying to get me to say anything. He gave me a container of pills and told me I could go home. I took it from him and opened the door.

My brother was sitting right outside the office. I wondered if he heard all what the doctor had said to me. I wondered what he was doing in the doctor's office but I didn't say anything to him apart from "The doctor said I can go home." We got some water from the receptionist at the hospital and I took two of the pills as per instructions. I didn't want to go home and face what was happening but I knew I had to. I asked James if we could sit and wait for a while for the medicine to stop the pain before we make our way home. He agreed. We sat on chairs outside the hospital building, not speaking about what had happened in the doctor's office. Instead, we sat there in silence staring at people and cars passing by. The silence said it all; I knew my brother knew something, even if not the full story. After a while the pain stopped, and we made our way home in silence, still no words between the two of us about what had just taken place.

My mother called my brother to find out what the doctor had said was the problem. I hoped he would make up a story and not tell the truth. I could hear my mother's voice at the side of the house, and assumed she was washing some clothes. I went to the back yard, sat on a piece of stone and was planning my escape route into the bushes. I must have been a thousand miles away in my mind because I didn't hear my mother's footsteps approaching. When I came to, she was standing right in front of me; I tried to hide my surprise, I was so scared. I didn't know what my brother had told her and I couldn't read much from her facial expressions.

I thought if she really knew, she'd be mad without trying to hide it. She sat next to me. I tried harder to compose myself. She asked me what the doctor had said. I showed her the medicine he gave me. She said "ah nuh dat mi ask yuh," and repeated the question. "Wah di doctor seh ah cause yuh belly fi hurt yuh?" I didn't know what to say. I definitely didn't want to lie to her if my brother had already told the truth, but I didn't want to be the one to say something, especially if she didn't suspect anything. I was confident that my life was over whether I spoke or not. For a slight moment it felt as if I'd lost my voice, because no words would come out when I opened my mouth. But the frustration on my mother's face was becoming unbearable and I knew what she'd do to me if I lied to her face, so I had to say something. I told her the doctor asked me if anyone was hurting me. She asked me what I said, I told her that I'd said no. So, she asked me why would the doctor ask me that? I told her that I didn't know, but she wasn't satisfied with my response. I thought she already knew, but she wanted to hear it from me. She kept asking who's troubling me, over and over and over until I finally responded by shouting "Ken! Ken a trouble mi!

I remember the deeply-hurt look in her eyes as they filled with tears instantly. I wasn't used to seeing my mother cry so easily, so it made it even more weird. She wiped her eyes and kept probing me for details: When? Where? How? etc. She didn't want to believe what I was saying to her. I knew this because she responded, "How him hold pon top ah yuh without crushing yuh?" I explained that he balanced some of his weight with his hands on the bed. She asked me how did he manage to get his thing inside me? I told her he kept trying. I answered all her questions and noticed she didn't respond as I'd thought. If anything, she seemed really worried and a bit confused. I started to feel a bit of hope for her. She told me not to tell him or anyone else about our conversation, and I thought to myself I dare not say a word. I guess over the next few days mum was planning our escape, because in less than a week, my mother was back at our family's house in Salt Spring with her five children.

Cottage Bottom

In Cottage Bottom, Montego Bay our closest family were spread out in three houses on a big piece of family land that stretched further than the eyes could see, although a lot of it was hills and gully. I've been told that my great grandmother on my mother's side Jucs (short for Jucella, aka Mama), had nine children. One of them, my mother's mother Nella,, passed away when my mother was only 10 years old, leaving her and her younger sister Patsy. My mother continued to live with Mama, and Aunt Patsy went to live with her father's family.

I've heard many wonderful stories about Nanna Nella being a brave, courageous and loving woman to everyone she came across. She had gone way too early, and according to many, at the hands of her partner Dave - Aunt Patsy's father. She was dearly missed by her family, entire community and especially her two daughters, who up this day, still cry for their mother.

I've been told that Nana Nella loved children dearly, and it would have been her very best wish to have met and be around her grandchildren. There's no picture of her for us to see. The best vision we have of her is by listening to some members of the family who say that my sister Joy is the living image and character of Nana Nella. She's no longer in her body, but her spirit lives on forever. Gone but never forgotten.

Of Mama's nine children, I grew up around only six of them; three boys and three girls. I loved Mama, she was like my Nan and I called her children Aunties and Uncles. Her three daughters, Aunties

Pam, Dolly & Mavis created separate homes on Mama's land, whilst the boys spread their wings. My (late) uncles Rupert and Brother lived further down on Cottage Bottom Road in separate homes with their families, whilst the eldest of all, my (late) Uncle Peter was the first to travel to the UK for work in the 1960's. I'm so grateful I got to know him a lot better as I grew older, but back then I only saw him briefly when he travelled to Jamaica on holidays.

Aunties Pam and Dolly lived in Mama's house with their families – our family home. Eventually this home became a mansion with several entrances, bedrooms and family spaces. Aunt Pam controlled the first half and Aunt Dolly had the second half which was built on a sloped hill and had a high staircase to enter the house from the back. At the front of the house was a huge veranda where many of our gatherings, memories and stories were created. A veranda is an open space at the front of the house, like a big balcony on the ground floor. I remember sitting on the veranda playing 'Supermario' on my late cousin Junior's 'gameboy'. I also remember combing Mama's hair and watching her sit peacefully as she looked out on the road in front of her.

Aunt Mavis had her own big house with several rooms, living room, kitchen, bathroom and veranda. She lived there with her own children. It always felt a little creepy in her house, but Aunt Mavis was always welcoming when we came to stay for short breaks.

Aunt Patsy built a two-bedroom house a short walk past Aunt Mavis' house. Around our family homes were lots of other houses, most of which I can't remember, but I do remember Miss Emin who lived right in front of Aunt Patsy's. We used to buy household items at her gate, and she had many big dogs; when they barked, I felt it in my bones, and hoped that gate would never open, or that they would never escape! I also remember Elvis's mansion right in front of Aunt Mavis's house. I remember Tanny and her children who lived between Aunt Mavis and Mama's house. There are other houses I can remember but find it more challenging to remember the people's names.

Most of the time, we all lived together as one community. I don't remember which families were related but we all looked out for each other, and all the children in the neighbourhood called the adults Aunties and Uncles.

There were various fruit and vegetable trees planted on Mama's land such as mangoes, naseburry, almond, pimento, plum and ackee trees. We also had a family graveyard under one of the naseburry trees where previous family members who'd passed away, rested. I had an experience one day in Mama's house when I was about 10 years old; I saw an image of Nana Nella through the window. Although I'd never had the pleasure of meeting her, I knew it was her, and I felt very familiar with her presence. In a split second she came and went, leaving me thinking that I was dreaming.

One of the things I really enjoyed was the freedom for all the children to play together from dawn until dusk each day, unless we had chores to do. If something went wrong in the group, I knew I was not alone, except if I was the one doing the wrong. If adults had to get involved, everyone would get a chance to say what happened, so the adults didn't just listen to one person. This was a great way to investigate and resolve disputes amongst us children, and we respected this culture.

Life here seemed so different to our home in Heskit – where I hardly played with anyone, including my own siblings. Being back home reminded me of lot of happy memories from my younger days, including playing (dolls) house with my cousins underneath the cellar of pur house, picking and washing naseburry with my great grandmother as well as chewing her chicken bones, which we used to compete with each other to get (you'd have to be there to understand this one), climbing trees, especially mango trees, as well as going on many adventures in the bushes.

I don't remember my mother or I telling anyone why we were there on this occasion; I suspected my mother just pulled it off as a normal holiday trip to see the family. I also don't remember my mother talking anymore to me about what I'd gone through with Ken. Instead, we all just seemed so happy to be back. What's more, in the short time we were there, I already had my eyes on one of my neighbour's sons called Mark.

Mark and I would spend days staring into each other's eyes from the comfort of our verandas. He sat on his dad's veranda whilst I sat on Aunt Mavis' and seeing as both homes were directly opposite each other, it became the perfect view for us to stare away at each other in the most romantic way. He was the first boy I looked at in this way, and I knew I liked him. One night, when all the children and young people gathered together, Mark took me aside and gave me my first real kiss. His lips were soft, tender and gentle. He taught me how to turn my head slightly to the left or right to connect my lips with his. I felt a deep connection with him, like safety, protection and love. I so badly wanted to share my burdens with him but was too afraid he would reject me if he knew, so I enjoyed what we shared and kept silent about everything else. I feared that word would get out about my stepdad and dreaded Mark asking me about it. I don't know if he knew or suspected anything, but the fact he never said anything made me so happy that I could keep this pure, innocent and undiluted love inside me.

Back into the Pit

My joy was cut short unexpectedly a few weeks later, when we had to return to Heskit, Negril. I didn't know why this was. I don't think anyone knew what was really going on except my mother who was under Ken's deep control, and kept quiet out of fear of being blamed, judged or making it worse. It was only when I got older, I became aware that Ken had travelled to Cottage Bottom and taken his three children back to his house, and that's why my mother felt she had to return there immediately. As an adult, I asked my mother why didn't she leave me with our family? She said she hadn't told them what had happened out of fear they wouldn't believe her, and without telling them, it would seem odd if she'd left me with them.

When we got back to the house in Heskit, my mother told me that I should tell her if Ken touched me again. But I was so angry with her for bringing me back into it; I thought to myself I would never trust her to tell her anything again. This was the second time I was making this promise to myself, but this time, I meant it more than ever! Why would I tell her anything after she'd clearly shown me, she couldn't protect me?! From that day on, I decided that to make life easier for myself, I would always give Ken what he wanted.

I expected Ken to be at war with my mother, but I wasn't sure how he felt about me. I didn't know if he knew the real reason why we'd left. But it seems he knew enough to understand that my mother had left him, which is why he'd come to get his kids. At the time I thought to myself that he must have known this would've instantly brought my mother back to him. Through the work I now do, I realised that perpetrators have many tactics they use to hold power and control over their victims. By Ken taking my mother's youngest children from her - his actions were much more intentional and dangerous than I can even imagine! Anyway, I decided to be on my best behaviour so as not to upset him any further. When he finally got to spend some time with me alone, I don't remember him asking me about breaking ***our*** secret, instead, he seemed more concerned and jealous over stories he must have heard about Mark and I. I was shocked. How did he find out about that? I had to quickly brush it off as nothing, and reassured him that I didn't even like Mark, and that nothing had happened between us. Anyway, he ended the conversation by kissing me and telling me how much he missed me. He also made me promise not to ever leave him again.

Gone But Never Forgotten

Shortly after this, tragic news travelled to us about my great grandmother in Cottage Bottom. We didn't have a telephone, so news normally reached us through letters or a human messenger by way of a family or friend. I'm unsure how this news was delivered but we heard that a fire broke out and burned down Mama's entire house – our family home. Everything was destroyed, including photographs and other family treasures. We were very grateful that everyone escaped unharmed, but Mama suffered two strokes, and as a result, died a few months later, at the age of around 88 years old. My last fun memory of her before she died, was when Tanny said to her "Mama, mi pregnant." Mama turned to her and said, "Ah mi breed yuh?" This made me laugh so much! I knew she wasn't well, but I was so glad to see her feisty character was still there.

We went to her funeral and I remember crying my eyes out. It was the first time I was losing someone so dear to me to death. Mark's support comforted me whilst I was there on this brief yet very painful occasion. Many family members travelled from England for the funeral, some I hadn't seen in a long time such as Aunt Pam, and some I'd never met before, such as Uncle Peter's children who were even older than me. It was a massive funeral and just about everyone from the neighbourhood and many others across Jamaica came to pay their last respects. I remember Aunt Pam gave me a £5 note and I was so excited, it felt like gold! lol.

Period Poverty

By age 12, I started to see my period. I didn't know it was normal for blood to come out of my vagina. I hated it. I hated the smell and the mess it made on my clothes. I hated how it made me feel about myself – disgusting! I hated the excruciating pain in my belly which reminded me of the other extreme belly pain I'd gone to the doctors for a couple of years earlier. It felt like I was being punished for allowing my stepdad to sexually abuse me. Each time my period came, I felt disgusted with myself and wished I didn't have to go through it. To make matters worse, I used to have to use toilet tissue, cloth or anything I could get my hands on. I knew money was tight at home, so I didn't want to be seen as a burden, nor did I want to tell my mother anything about me. But in the end, I decided I couldn't keep it to myself. I needed help. When I told her, she instructed me where in the house I could find the money to buy pads and painkillers from our local shop, owned my Mr Ainsley. I had to walk about 20 minutes each way in pain, but I had to go and get what I needed.

My 'Best Friend' Shorty

Ken continued molesting me whenever he wanted. Sometimes it was as frequent as weekly, other times a few months would pass, and nothing would happen. It seemed random. I could never predict when it would happen next, so I was always on the alert and 'ready' for him, just in case. This meant he was in my mind all the time. I started to have strong feelings for him again. I was torn. I didn't want to like him, but I couldn't help myself, so I blamed my mother all over again. I rebelled against her harsh discipline. I felt I was a woman now, so why should I still be treated like a little girl? Moreover, I had made friends with a girl a few years older than me who had recently moved down the road with her family. We called her Shorty as she was so beautiful, short and funny. I enjoyed her company, but what I enjoyed more was seeing the relationship she had with her mother. They were like best friends who respected each other and even when they fell out, they made back up in no time, like nothing ever happened. She told me that she tells her mother everything, which was the complete opposite to me and my mother because I only told her what I had to. Shorty and I became really close over the next few months, telling each other secrets, except about Ken. I wouldn't dare tell anyone else about Ken!

I thought the reason why we connected so easily was because she knew what it was like to have a tough upbringing. As an older girl, she could see my struggles and wanted to help. Me on the other hand needed an escape, a friend, someone I could trust and offload so many things packed up in my mind. I thought she was really humble and sweet. We talked and laughed a lot, mostly about boys and other girly stuff, which was refreshing, seeing as I had no-one to have these conversations with, since I'd fallen out with my best friend Antonnette from school. I complained a lot to her about my mother and the horrible ways I thought my mother treated me. "Mi tink she have something against mi. Mi no think she even like me and mi hate live wid har!" I'd say to Shorty, complaining about my mother. Shorty's mother often intervened in the conversation to let me know that she understood where I was coming from, and if I ever needed somewhere to go, I could stay with them. This kind of support from Shorty and her mother was so overwhelming! I couldn't get enough so I tried to spend all of my free time with them.

As soon as my mother would leave the yard, I would sneak out to Shorty's house and I'd usually come back just in time before my mother got back. A few times my cover was blown, and she'd know I'd been to Shorty's house; she'd shout at me and tell me how much of a bad influence Shorty was on me. She was convinced that Shorty would "lead me astray" which means they'd encourage me to do bad things. I obviously didn't agree. I thought they treated me like the responsible adult that I am (or that I thought I was considering I was barely 13 years old).

Spanish Fly

"Rape is one type of sexual violence. Sexual violence is the general term we use to describe any kind of unwanted sexual act or activity." [17]

"The legal definition of rape is 'penetration with a penis of the vagina, anus or mouth of another person without their consent.

---

17 https://rapecrisis.org.uk/get-help/looking-for-information/what-is-sexual-violence/what-is-rape/

Sexual consent is when we agree by choice, and have the freedom and capacity to make that choice.

That means that someone cannot give their consent when they are:

- *Scared or threatened*
- *Bullied*
- *Very drunk or under the influence of drugs*
- *Asleep"* [18]

One night my mother beat me really bad. I don't remember what I'd (supposedly) done this time, but I do remember her saying to me that I should "come out of har house." I've come to understand this is a general thing for Jamaican mothers to say to their children. However, I saw this as a real opportunity to get out and be around people that actually liked me! "She nuh affi tell mi twice!" I thought. I quickly ran out of the yard and ran to Shorty's house. I was a mess – in tears, pain and bruises from the beatings. Shorty and her mother quickly comforted me. They said nice words to me such as, "hush darling, yuh nuh deserve dis. No, sah, yuh mumma shouldn't do dis to yuh!" They hugged me, comforted me and offered me somewhere to stay for the night. They gave me a drink and sat down with me to talk.

I remember telling them what had happened that night why I was in trouble with my mother, but of course I was telling them from **my** perspective, which meant I was right and she was wrong. I also remember one of Shorty's cousins coming over to their house – his name was Weston and he lived directly opposite my house with his mother, step-dad and two brothers. I used to like one of his younger brothers, although I wasn't sure if he liked me too. Nevertheless, I knew nothing could ever happen because it was too close to home

18 https://rapecrisis.org.uk/get-help/looking-for-information/what-is-sexual-violence/what-is-rape/

with Ken watching over me. I think Weston's step-dad was related to Ken. Weston was well known in the neighbourhood and a very good Christian man at church. He was also eye candy amongst all the ladies because he was tall, dark and handsome. It was normal in Jamaica for people to have pet names; Weston's pet name was 'Donkey Man', because of the size of his penis.

Weston came and sat next to me and was comforting me in that moment. Instantly, I felt special and thought that he cared. The last thing I remember was Shorty and her mother getting up to go into the next room. I wouldn't have been too concerned because I completely trusted the environment. If anything, I continued to feel special the more time I spent with him. "Did he like me? Why was he spending so much time with me?" I was confused. I didn't have all the answers, but I didn't care too much at the time. I was just glad he was giving me his undivided attention at my time of need.

The next thing I knew, I woke up the next morning on the bed covered in blood! I froze for a few minutes lying there, then thought that maybe my period had come whilst I was asleep. I felt ashamed, disgusted and started thinking how was I going to explain this to Shorty and her mother? I got up off the bed and saw the blood all over my clothes. The blood smelled horrible. My belly really hurt which made me believe even more that it was my period, although I wasn't expecting it at this time. One thing was different; my vagina felt sore. I couldn't explain that to myself. I also realized I couldn't remember anything that had happened after Shorty and her mother left me in the room with Weston. My mind was absolutely blank. I was confused, scared, and frightened. How could I have forgotten everything after that point? Did I just fall asleep whilst talking to Weston?

It started to really bother me, and then I thought I'd speak to Shorty about it. When I went in the other room, she wasn't there but her mother was. Her mother didn't seem to know what had happened to me, but she said Shorty had gone to the shop. She told me to go home and get myself cleaned up and she'll take care of the bed. I was a bit relieved how calmly she was taking it.

To avoid anyone seeing me, I cut through the bushes to get home and entered from the back of our house. I hoped my mum or Ken would be out because, for different reasons, I couldn't bear either of them seeing me in that state. When I got home, I was so glad that neither of them was there. I could hear my siblings playing in the front yard. I kept a very low-profile cleaning myself up.

The Aftermath

I noticed the bleeding had stopped which I thought was so weird because if it was my period, I'd be bleeding for days. "So, how did it happen?" I questioned myself. As I washed my vagina using my rag (aka flannel), I noticed how tender and painful it was. I became convinced something had happened to me at Shorty's house, but that's all I was certain of. Everything else was going around and round in my head; "Did Shorty and her mother know what happened? Did it have anything to do with Weston? Why can't I remember? What if my mother and/ or Ken finds out?" I was so distressed with worry and didn't have anyone to talk to. I kept looking out all day expecting Shorty to stop by my house or send me a message. I thought when she got back home and found out about the blood, she'd want to check to see if I'm ok, but she never came. Two days passed and still no Shorty. I sneaked out of my yard to visit her but yet again her mother said she wasn't home. My mind was blown away still trying to figure out what had happened to me, but even more so, wanting to know if Shorty had anything to do with it.

I decided to write a letter to release all the thoughts going around in my head. I didn't want my mother to see me writing and become curious, so I went further down in the yard, away from our house and hid behind a huge mango tree stump. At first, I didn't know if I was actually writing to anyone, but then a thought came to me to write to the pastor of my church. He was the only one I could think of that may really want to help and who I could trust. It also made sense, seeing as Ken sang in the church choir and I was a member of the church.

So, I kept writing, letting it all out – but then suddenly my mother unexpectedly approached me from behind! The shock of it made my heart race into my mouth! I thought "dat's it, mi life over now!" I expected my mother to take the letter from me immediately. Instead she said she had come to see what I was doing, and now she realises I'm writing a letter, she wants to be the first to read it after I'm done. She left me to continue writing with the expectation that I'd bring it straight to her when I'd finished. My nerves were killing me. What should I do? If I brought it to her, she'll know exactly what I thought had happened to me the night I left her house to go to Shorty's. If I didn't give it to her, she'd know I'm hiding something and will interrogate me until it comes out, then beat the hell out of me. Either way, I couldn't bear what the outcome might be. All I kept thinking was that I couldn't bring myself to give the letter to my mother. So, I decided to run into the bushes and get rid of the letter. I also planned to write another letter quickly, but if I didn't get the chance, I was going to tell my mother "the wind blew it away". I felt much better now that I had a plan. Even if it wasn't properly executed and I got into trouble, it was still better than getting into trouble for what was actually in the letter.

So, I ran as fast as I could into the bushes without looking behind me. I kept running until something said I should stop. I took the letter out from my pocket and started tearing it up in order to scatter it in that part of the bushes. As I was tearing it into finer pieces, my mother appeared and ordered me to give it to her. I kept tearing it up, knowing full well that it would only add to my troubles. But I was willing to risk anything if my mother never found out what was in the letter. Unfortunately, she lurched towards me and grabbed the pieces of paper from my hand. It happened so fast that there was nothing I could've done about it. She tried to piece the papers back together while I stood there frozen; she read my very personal letter, against all my efforts. My nightmare was playing out right in front of my eyes and there was nothing I could do about it. I felt completely helpless. The best I could hope for was that the papers were too badly torn for her to see what was written on them.

After a few minutes, she raised her head from the letter and looked up at me. Her face seemed different. She started asking me what had happened, which annoyed me because I thought she already knew. At first, I tried to be vague, referring her back to my letter she had in her hands. She started hitting me in my head and across my back and shoulder for me to tell her what happened between Weston and I. As she called his name, I thought I'd better tell her in case she thought I wanted it.

I was terrified and was instantly reminded of the time when I was five years old, where Uncle Benny had tried to molest me; my mother had threatened to pepper and salt my vagina if she ever found out about me and another guy. She didn't do it when she found out about Ken because she probably knew it wasn't my fault, but if she thought for a second that I wanted it with Weston, it could make her go back on her promise. I thought I'd rather die than to have that happen to me after everything I'd just been through.

I started to talk and tell her everything I knew. My mother got so angry! She stormed out of the bushes towards our house. I didn't know what she was going to do. I didn't want Ken to find out as he kept telling me "Nuh giv weh mi something." A small part of me even worry that this may make Ken reject me. I was in so much of an emotional turmoil and didn't know what to do. I stayed in the bushes for hours – too scared to return to reality. By the time I returned to the house, it was already starting to get dark. Everyone had already eaten dinner and it was my night to wash the dishes. I remember washing them and headed straight to bed.

Public Humiliation

"Public humiliation is related to embarrassment, but is typically longer-lasting and more painful.. People experiencing humiliation may have diminished feelings of self-worth.. and is characterized as a desire to hide or escape. Public humiliation sometimes occurs with trauma.. such as rape." [19]

The next day, I woke up feeling like there was a huge rock on top of me. I didn't know if my mother had said anything or what she was going to do. I didn't want to get out of bed, but I had to go to school. After school, my mother quietly told me she'd been to the police station and reported what Weston had done to me. I was blown away by her revelation. I couldn't believe she had taken it that far, considering what Ken had been doing to me for years, and still no police were involved. What did she hope to achieve by going to the police? Now everyone would know, and it would just be my word against his. I hadn't heard from Shorty or her mother since that night, and I didn't feel they would choose my side over their cousin's. I couldn't bear thinking about going over it all with

19 https://www.goodtherapy.org/blog/psychpedia/humiliation

the police. I thought no-one would believe me anyway. Every time I thought my life couldn't get any worse, it did. My mother tried to reassure me that it was the right thing to do. I couldn't tell her all the thoughts that were in my mind because I didn't want it to seem like I was going against her, or like I was trying to protect Weston. So, I just nodded and went along with her advice. Within the next two weeks, everything changed and got even worse. I had to go to the police station and confirm what I'd written in my letter, as my mother had handed it over to them after taping it back together. I heard that Weston also had to give his statement and somehow everyone in the neighbourhood found out. My life was never the same again.

People made nasty remarks and threw stones when I walked past their house or they passed me on the road. No-one at school wanted to talk to me. I felt alone and completely rejected in the community for something that wasn't even my fault. By this time, it was said that Weston or Shorty had put "Spanish Fly" in my drink to make me go to sleep, and then Weston had raped me. This was a common thing we'd hear would happen to 'stray' girls. So, it made complete sense as to why I couldn't remember anything. But to this day it doesn't make sense why Shorty, my best friend at the time, would allow something like that to happen to me. Why would Weston want to do that to me when he could get any girl he wanted? If he'd asked me, I probably would have said yes, who knows?! Was it a coincidence that Weston turned up there that same night I left my mother's house? Was it planned? There were too many unanswered questions that filled my mind and to top it all off, I couldn't deal with the shame and disgrace from everyone knowing. Plus, I was getting the 'silent treatment' from Ken, so it worried me not knowing where I stood with him, or how he felt about the police involvement. Would he be next? Was his secret out of the bag? All this played on my mind, causing me even greater anxiety. It didn't seem as if my mother had thought through the implications of going to the police, or how Ken would respond to it. I know she was very scared of Ken, so if she had thought for a second that this would have angered him in any way, she wouldn't have gone.

A few months later, I had to go to court in Negril. I was told I'd have to sit on the stand in front of everyone and give my account of what happened to me. I dreaded that moment but knew I didn't have a choice. But then the day before, my mother told me she's withdrawing the case because she ran out of money. I was livid; I felt like I couldn't breathe. All I could think was "How dare you!" Although I was relieved that I didn't have to take the stand, I was more upset about the fact that now everyone knew, and by withdrawing the case, it made it look like I was lying on Weston all along. I couldn't take my life anymore. I felt battered all over and I knew it wouldn't end there.

I held my head down as I walked down the road; people shouted insults at me when I walked past them, whispering to each other about me, shouting at me to drop the case, people were saying I wanted it, and it's only because my mother found out why I was saying he raped me; the public humiliation affected me to my core, affecting my value, self-worth, how I perceived myself and my entire world around me. It caused social anxiety e.g. extreme nervousness in social situations, feeling that everyone is judging me, having everyone else's thoughts in my head as opposed to my own thoughts. The only thing that kept me going was that I still found some comfort in my religious beliefs and my education. Having said that, I stopped going to church for a while in order to avoid seeing him, but when we did cross paths, he often had a smirking smile on his face.

In retrospect, I now realize that as Ken controlled the finances, it would have cost a lot of money to bring a case like this to court, and my mother would have had to rely on him for the funds. He obviously didn't want me to win the case because if I was to win, what would stop me from coming after him next? He wouldn't have wanted me to bring this attention to our home, because of the chance that what he was doing to me could also become public knowledge.

My Fighting Streak

I was still getting into serious fights at school and was at risk of getting excluded. Once I got sent home for slapping a teacher in the face because she tried to stop me from hitting a boy. Another time I got suspended from school for a week after putting a girl in hospital. This girl had been troubling me for some time; I wasn't scared of her because she was skinny, but many of her family members also attended our school, so I tried my best to avoid getting into anything with her. But one day in the playground, she took her jokes too far and hit me in the face. My mother always told me not to be scared to defend myself, as long as I didn't hit them first. So, I completely lost it with the girl, and then she got all her family at the school to beat me up. By the time they were done, my clothes were ragged on me and I could hardly stand up. Some of the children picked me up and brought me to my house, which was less than a 5-minute walk down the road. The rest of the school children followed behind us because they didn't want to miss my mother's response.

My mother was at home washing clothes when she heard the huge uproar coming towards the yard. She went to the gate and saw the children holding me up on both sides. They shouted out that Annie from school had gotten her family to beat me up. My mother grabbed hold of one of my hands and pulled me to stand up. She said "We ah guh get Annie now!" My mother marched off with me behind, and the rest of the children followed us closely back to the school. As we approached the school, I could see Annie still in the playground with her family. I pointed them out to my mother. She told me to go and beat up any one of them I choose. Seeing us coming towards them, Annie ran into the school building; I chased her, my mother ran after me and everyone else ran behind us. Annie was known for her speed on sports days but I chased her all over the school until she finally tripped over and I jumped on her. After beating her up my mother pulled me off her and told me that's enough now. My mother then left the school saying I should come and get her if anyone else touched me. After my mother left, the teachers found me and brought me to the Principal's office. I was suspended for a week and missed a long-planned school trip I was really looking forward to.

At home I often got into fights with my brothers and sisters too. I can remember scratching up my brother James's neck with my fingernails, which were one of my key fighting techniques; anytime I fought, I would always drew people's blood with my bare hands; I was a lioness before I even knew it!

Joy and I didn't have a good relationship until well into our adult life. I was jealous of her and didn't like her because I thought she was selfish with her toys. One day Aunty Patsy came to visit and brought two dolls for us, Joy got the skinny (white) doll with long hair and I got the short-haired (black) doll. I thought Joy was the favourite and that's why she got the "better one". I couldn't understand what I was meant to do with a short-haired doll, so I threw mine away. Although Joy wasn't fussed about playing with her new doll, she wouldn't allow me to play with it either.

We competed for everything but what made me hate Joy even more, was my mother would always call her to find something to beat me with. It could be a shoe, belt, stick, anything and Joy seemed all too happy to get her exactly what she needed. Talking this over with Joy years later, she told me she too was scared of our mother, and didn't want the anger turned on her if she didn't do exactly as she was told.

My First Love

Soon it was time to choose which High School I wanted to attend. My first choice was Mannings High School in Sa-va-na-la Mar, but when the time came to do the entrance exams, I missed it due to another trip back to our family home in Cottage Bottom. I was very disappointed to miss this opportunity because getting a good education meant I could get a good job and finally leave home. But now I had to wait an extra year for my escape! However, I was glad I got to see Mark again, and we made sure we spent as much of our time together hugging, kissing, talking and holding hands. He was the only one I trusted at the time and I craved his company more and more. Considering we spent so little time together (i.e whenever I came to visit), I think I felt like that because he was the only person I actually ***chose*** to be around. Everyone else was there because of some other reason such as family, neighbours, school mates, church brothers and sisters, etc. I just liked the way I felt so normal and un-judged around him. He was a handsome, popular and romantic black boy in my age group who seemed to genuinely enjoy my company; he didn't seem to want anything more which was against everything I'd learnt for myself by that time. He was my first love.

Frank

My family returned back home just before the summer holidays ended and a close family friend Frank came back with us for a little while. Frank was older than me but younger than my brother James; he was tall, brown and muscular with dimples that formed in his cheeks when he smiled. Everyone liked Frank as he was always playful and fun to be around. Ken had built a further two rooms to our house, which meant we had three bedrooms and one living room. My mother and Ken shared one room with my new baby sister; whilst the boys and girls were split up in individual rooms: I was with my other two younger sisters whilst James was with my younger brother Mikel, so naturally Frank would have slept in James' room. But one night when everybody was asleep, he crept into my room and came into my bed. I didn't think anything of it, so I didn't question him to find out what he was doing there, instead I moved over so he could get in the bed and lay at the front. We whispered to each other in the dark until I was dozing off.

I woke up with my back turned to Frank; his hands were holding my waist as he tried to poke his penis through my legs from behind. I felt this pointy, warm and hard thing coming through my legs. At first, I was worried and confused. It reminded me of waking up in the same position to what Uncle Benny was trying to do, except it seemed Frank was much further ahead in his actions. He seemed really into what he was doing and didn't seem to care about how much movement he was making under the covers, or if he woke anyone else up.

My body felt receptive to his touches. I guess by this time, I was well experienced in these kinds of activities. And because of what Ken was already doing to me, I didn't feel the need to stop Frank. [20] I soon

20 In studies of revictimization.. there is general agreement on the increased risk of

started to feel relaxed under the covers with him. I knew exactly what he was doing was wrong, but I let him because I was starting to enjoy it. I didn't turn around or anything, nor did I try to stop him. I lay there quietly enjoying it as his penis entered my vagina. He started to breathe really heavily, and in a split second I felt warm liquid dripping on my bum and my thighs. After this, the movement stopped in the bed and he seemed to have fallen asleep. I lay there feeling ashamed, yet wanting more. My body wasn't ready to sleep yet, it seemed to have its own urges beyond my control. I felt my fingers moving towards my vagina as I caressed around it until I finally felt a sense of relief. I was ok to go to sleep now.

When I woke up the next morning, Frank wasn't in my bed and I never spoke of it until now. I don't remember anything changing in the way we played together as children, except I did feel slightly awkward around him after that day, but I blocked it out because I believed it would cause much more worry that it's worth. I also thought that if Ken could get away with what he'd been doing to me all those years, then what Frank did was nothing compared to that.

The ongoing situation with Ken was diminishing my self-worth, and led to me becoming promiscuous as the years went on. Having said that, I just couldn't get my head around the fact that by 13 years old, I'd had so many different sexual partners and experiences, all without my expressed consent. I knew enough to know this wasn't normal, so I thought something must be wrong with ***me***. If my past experiences were anything to go by, it was clear to me that I was cursed and destined for a life of failure and mis-haps. But yet something inside me kept fighting, even when I thought I'd given up and didn't see the point anymore.

---

revictimization for victims of childhood abuse (Barnes, Noll, Putnam, & Trickett, 2009; Stefansen & Mossige, 2007; Widom, Czaja, & Dutton, 2008; https://www.tandfonline.com/doi/full/10.1080/14043858.2019.1568103)

Brain Box

After the summer holidays ended, I went back to school and tried to stay away from any problems, even though it felt like trouble followed me wherever I went. My grades were good, especially in Maths, my best subject. My Maths teacher, Mr Johnson used to push me in a way that allowed me to thrive beyond my understanding. One of the best things he would do, was when he set the class a mathematical problem, he would give us about a minute to figure it out; then would then go around the whole class to hear the answer, and how we had worked it out. He always left me for last because he knew that 9 times out of 10, I'd come up with the correct answer but with a completely different way of working it out. Sometimes it seemed I surprised my teacher by presenting a new way of working out a mathematical problem that he hadn't thought of – although he never really admitted it. My mind became my greatest asset and at the same time, the home of my greatest nightmares!

The time came to choose which schools I wanted to apply for. I chose Mannings High School as my top choice and Frome Tec College was my second choice. Although my brother James went to Frome, I really wanted to go to Mannings because it had an exceptional reputation for producing high quality students, and only the best was allowed to attend. I focused really hard on my exams and prayed consistently asking God for this one wish to come true. I started going to church again, but this time I wanted to go even more frequently so I could be in the presence of God, and be able to communicate with Him. However, I was limited to going on Wednesday evenings and Saturdays only, because of other responsibilities at home. At first, I wasn't happy about this limitation because I thought my mother just wanted to control me, so I complained to my pastor. The pastor spoke to my mother and then explained to me that my mother had promised to allow me to attend every Wednesday and Saturday, but on the other days my mother needed my help at home. I didn't fight it. Instead I found comfort in knowing that every Wednesday evening and all-day Saturdays I'd be out of the house and in God's presence. After completing my exams, it was the waiting game that made me anxious. I had very little belief I would get what I wanted, but I was still hoping. I saw this as my one chance of getting out of the horrific life I was living. Finally, the news came – I got into Mannings! Words still can't express my excitement when I found out. In fact, everybody seemed surprised, yet genuinely happy for me. I remember my mother being the happiest and proudest I'd seen her in as far back as I could remember.

Flanker

After the excitement died down, reality hit my mother that she would need money to buy all the things I'd need for a new school, including uniform, shoes, bag, books etc. She told me she didn't have the money but I knew that wouldn't stop me. She said she would send me to my father's house in Flanker, Montego Bay for me to get money from my dad. Up to this point, I was never aware of receiving any money from my dad for anything but I agreed it was worth a try.

At the beginning of the summer holidays, my mother gave James and I money to go to our father's house to get money from him. My father lived in a two-bedroom house with his wife and four daughters, as well as his step-daughter Tina (his wife's eldest daughter she had with another man before they got married). His wife's parents also lived there in separate extensions on the property. The house was built on lots of huge rocks. As you stepped out of the house, you had to be very careful not to cut your foot or fall on the rocks. I hated his wife because I believed she treated all of her children more favorably than me, even though I was older than all of them – except Tina. I remember one time she cooked a pot of hard food (dumplings and potatoes) with stew chicken. She gave all her children more dumplings than me and I never got over that. I didn't get on with Tina because for most of the time, I thought she was miserable and no fun at all. I got on better with all of my sisters, especially Collette and ***Little (RIP)***. Sasha was the baby in the family at the time, and they looked after her. Little and Mampy were twins. I was so envious of the special bond they all seemed to share because I didn't have that with anyone. Sometimes I felt like they treated me differently, like I wasn't one of them. For example, secret jokes they shared and wouldn't let me in. It wasn't until I got older that I realized when it came down to it, we were all in the same boat there. In fact, they were probably more jealous of James and I because the few times we visited, we always looked good and when my mother came for us, she would give them food and money. I also remember my other brother Dwayne and sister Kadian. They both had separate mothers and lived different lifestyles but when they came to visit our dad, we were all in the same boat.

Food Poverty vs Hunger

"Food poverty is the inability of individuals and households to obtain an adequate and nutritious diet." [21]

"In politics, humanitarian aid, and social science, hunger is a condition in which a person, for a sustained period, is unable to eat sufficient food to meet basic nutritional needs." [22]

I remember one of the neighbours had a plum tree and some of the branches would hang to the left side of our yard. We'd be glad when the plums fell off the tree. They were big, juicy and delicious. On the other side of the yard lived a family friend we called Kitty. He lived there with his girlfriend. They fed us many times and were good to us, especially my brother James – they seemed to take a particular liking to him so we used that to our advantage. At times when we didn't have anything to eat, we would send James to ask Kitty for food. Sometimes James would eat off the food and come back saying he didn't get any, when it was apparent from the bits on his face! This would just make us even more frustrated. We would then turn to begging people in the area but if we really couldn't get any food, I'd resort to picking up drink

21 https://www.london.gov.uk/what-we-do/business-and-economy/food/our-projects-food-london/food-poverty-action-plans
22 https://en.m.wikipedia.org/wiki/Hunger

bottles from the street and selling them in shops. The way I saw it, this was better than sitting down hopeless on my hungry belly.

As long as we had enough to buy flour and/or rice, I knew we were ok because we could eat it with butter or ketchup. If we had more money, we'd buy cheap meat such as chicken, salt fish, tinned mackerel, sardines or tuna. Whatever we got to eat; we'd make it last until the next meal time where we may have to repeat this process all over again.

I came to understand that we should never have had to live that life considering my dad worked as a builder and mechanic. He was constantly on long term contracts and therefore always had money, but he was very irresponsible, had terrible habits and bad money management skills. My mother often said he was a "useless good fi nothing, excuse of a man." When I was there, I noticed he was only at home on the weekends because his job required him to work away from home. I often heard his wife cursing that my dad would receive his pay check each Friday when he got released from work, yet we didn't see him until Saturday nights, if we were lucky. His wife often heard stories about my dad partying and having fun with young girls, wasting away all his money. By the time he came home, his wife would be cursing and fighting him over money. Apparently, she would take any money he had left which he usually said was to get him back to work the next day. This carried on every week. I was probably there for about four weeks which was the longest I'd ever stay there for – although it seemed like forever. Days and nights would pass with my belly rumbling with hunger. Even my birthday came and went with no acknowledgement; I'd pray that my mother would come and bring us back home.

I was the happiest person alive to see my mother when she finally arrived – she was surprised to see how much weight I'd lost.

When I asked my mother what took her so long, she explained that because she didn't have money, she had to wait to get some. I assumed that Ken gave it to her but later found out that a family friend had also contributed. Nevertheless, she raised enough money to be able to come and take James and I back home, as well as buying me all the things I needed for my new school – all except a new pair of shoes. My mother assured me that it wouldn't be long before she would get more money to buy me the shoes. She pleaded with me to stay home and wait for the shoes before I start school. But I was way too excited, determined and committed to start my new school and continue with my education, to let a pair of shoes get in my way. I tried on my old shoes to see if they could work. My toes were hanging out the front of both shoes, but I still wore them on my first day at school.

Mannings High School

On my first day at High School, needless to say the other kids made fun of my toes hanging out but I didn't care. I was focused on my goal and that's all that mattered to me. That goal was to leave home as quickly as possible, and getting a good education was my way of doing so. Besides, attending Mannings gave me a new sense of freedom and independence, which made me feel good about myself. For the first time, I was travelling on my own, taking a bus and a taxi to school. It was the first time I was allowed to travel so far alone, and I loved it; I loved the new sense of independence and freedom it gave me. It took me just over an hour to get to school each day. I soon recognized the fun and popular buses most of the school children travelled in together; my favourite was ***Bimmer***. Not only was it fun, I also wanted to ride amongst the most popular children. They played very loud dancehall music and bantered a lot. The bus was always over packed with school children – each person sitting on another person's lap. Being amongst this crowd boost my self-esteem and I wanted so much to be like "one of them". The school premises were massive from the front gate; it had many different buildings that looked the same. I was used to going to a school which only had one building. There were so many children all dressed in the same uniform – blue skirt and white top. Everyone's shoes looked clean and neat on their feet – all except mine. I tried to walk fast or distract people's attention so they didn't focus on my shoes. That didn't really work especially when we sat down in class and everyone stared at my shoes. I felt the children were a bit mean but maybe I'd have been the same if I was them. Overall my first impression of High School was overwhelming. I couldn't believe that someone like me had gotten into this amazing school when others more fortunate than I, had tried tirelessly without success. My favorite subjects were Maths and Spanish. My favorite teacher was Miss Marshall.

Planning to Escape

"Every individual in an abusive relationship needs a safety plan. Plans should cover your specific needs at different times in the cycle of the abusive relationship (and particularly around planning to escape when the risks increases). [23]

Soon after starting High School, my mother came to me with a plan to finally escape Ken for good. I'd dreamt of my mother rescuing us from Ken for so long that I'd completely given up on this possibility. The only way I saw out was doing it myself through education. My worst nightmare at the time was the possibility of getting pregnant for Ken. I wouldn't know what I'd do with myself, apart from watching all my dreams drift away, leaving me stuck in that situation.

After my mother's last failed attempt running to our family in Cottage Bottom, I didn't realize she still had it in her to try again. I mean, I understood ***why*** she wanted to escape and free her children too, because Ken was still beating her terribly on a regular basis and, I assumed my mother suspected that Ken was still molesting me, even though she never said another word to me about it. Furthermore, when Ken beat any of us children including me, it was like our last day on this earth.

Whilst mum would beat us for each wrongdoing at the time, Ken would batter us like he was fighting some monster on the road. He called it "adding up your ounces til they reached a pound". Once he beat Joy so badly for losing his $500.00 that many neighbours came to beg him and cried real tears when he wouldn't listen to

---

23 https://www.reducingtherisk.org.uk/cms/content/safety-planning. For more information on creating a safety plan, visit https://www.womensaid.org.uk/the-survivors-handbook/making-a-safety-plan/

them.At the time, he also had two of his older children at the house; they tried to plead with him too, but without success. Another time he almost knocked me unconscious after wrongfully accusing me of stealing money from the new grocery shop, he'd opened with a couple of his friends. I hadn't even seen the money because I was too busy stealing sweets from the shop instead.

I was excited by my mother's new plans of escaping because it indicated to me that she still wanted out and hadn't given up. However, I thought that these plans were particularly impossible. My mother was planning to escape to England to stay with our family there, and to send for us to join her. I'd long dreamed of England from when my Aunt Pam went years ago. I remember she had written to my mother, before we moved to Heskit, asking for me to join her, but my mother had declined. Now here we were discussing the possibility of this dream coming true. As excited as I was, I didn't want to leave Mannings High School or my first love Mark, though I knew England was a better option.

My mother told me of her plans to raise the money by joining a pardner – this was a very common and effective way to raise money in Jamaica. Each person within a group pays a fixed amount of money each month to the 'banker', and each month one person gets their draw – which is the total amount paid in that month, minus bankers fees, or any other deductions. There are general rules around pardners; and each banker may make up their own additional rules. A good example of this is: a group of 5 people select one person as the banker. Each person agrees to give the banker £300 each month for 5 months. Month one, one person gets their "draw" of £1,500 (minus banker's fee). The person receiving their draw would have to carry on paying £300 a month until the end. Month two, the second person gets the same draw, and it carries on until month 5. The downfall is, some people can't be trusted and may stop paying in their monthly contribution once they get their draw, which then affects all other draws after theirs. I've heard that pardner is illegal is England, but it wasn't in Jamaica when we were there. I don't know how much my mother had to contribute each month in her pardner, but she clearly did very well in hiding it from Ken.

My mother also told me of a close family friend who would be coming to Jamaica soon, and would return to England in March 1999. The plan was for my mother to go with the lady upon her return. So now my mother had a date in mind and a good plan.

We also spoke about how she would obtain her documents without Ken finding out. She needed my help with this and I happily helped her at every step of the way, without saying anything to anyone. After she bought her ticket, she told Ken that her family had offered her a brief holiday in England, and she'd be back in two weeks. I knew she wasn't planning to come back. It was sad and painful to say goodbye to her, although I knew she was going to pave a better path for her children.

On this final attempt, my mother successfully escaped a severely violent and abusive partner. Unlike her other attempts, this occasion was carefully planned and thoroughly thought through. She was out of the country and Ken didn't suspect a thing. He wasn't threatened that she was leaving him especially as it wasn't a reaction to a recent fight and she'd left all her children behind. It was one of the best yet most riskiest escape plans I've ever heard of.

Girly

When my mother was leaving Jamaica, she made arrangements for me to stay with a family friend called Miss Bev. Miss Bev is one of the three siblings that lived on the land we used to live in Mount

Airy (before we moved to Heskit). Miss Bev was a mature woman with grand-children a few years older than me. She lived in a big house made of wood and concrete with two of her grand-children (a pair of twin girls Patrice and Petra), two of her sons and her boyfriend. Although I looked up to and even envied the twins for their bond, my relationship with them was very temperamental at the time (although we're now good friends).

I knew Miss Bev to be a nice but firm woman. I'd encountered a previous bad experience one evening at her house when her son caught me stealing the drinks she used to make "suck suck" (aka bag juice). Trying to avoid getting into trouble, I lied to her and my mother. After inspecting my mouth, it was very clear to them that I was lying, and so that evening I got a good beating from my mother. But it wasn't her fault and I didn't really hold it against her.

At first, I was glad to leave the home we shared with Ken to go and stay with Miss Bev. But soon afterwards, I started missing my own home for two main reasons. Firstly, Miss Bev started to wrongfully accuse me of wanting her boyfriend: One day I was sat in her backyard and decided to make myself useful in her home. Without anyone telling me to, I picked up a broom and started sweeping the dining room. The broom knocked against the wooden part of the house, making loud noises. I was oblivious to any impact this may've had, but Miss Bev to stormed into the dining room to see where the noise was coming from. Upon seeing me, she instantly started accusing me of purposefully making the noise in order to attract attention from her boyfriend who was "sleeping" in the room next door. I was gob smacked by this revelation, as that accusation was completely beyond me! For starters, her boyfriend was an old man with grey hair and missing teeth and certainly not attractive in my eyes. I was gutted to be caught up in this rumor, remembering how it felt when everyone accused me of "***lying about being raped***."

To my knowledge, they didn't know about Ken. If they were to ever find out, surely, they'd think I was lying about Ken too, or maybe they'd think I wanted it, I reasoned within myself. The worse case scenario is that my mother told Miss Bev about Ken, and she indirectly used it against me. I thought my reputation was beyond repair and everyone would believe her over me, especially because she was a mature woman and I was just a child. I tried to defend myself and tell her the truth, but she already knew me to be a liar so she didn't believe a word I said. Over the next few days, she would randomly lashed out at me in front of anyone, and brought back up the accusation about her boyfriend. This meant I was constantly reliving that pain.

Miss Bev would also say that my mother had left me without any money to look after me. However, when I spoke to my mother over the phone, she told me how much money she'd already sent Miss Bev, so I knew she was lying about that. But it felt like I was living another nightmare. It wasn't until another lady who lived next to Miss Bev told me that she was a jealous and mean woman and often accused other women and girls of wanting to steal her boyfriend. The lady told me of various scenarios where she'd done the same thing that she was doing to me. I felt some relief, knowing that I wasn't alone and at least one person believed me. It wasn't nice living there, but I felt I had to. As I got older, I heard many other people complaining about Miss Bev accusing them of wanting her boyfriend. This included married women and her own family members. It's clear she was insecure about herself but that doesn't excuse her negatively impacting other people's lives with her lies, especially as her man wasn't easy even on the eyes.

One day on my way back from school, an ambulance passed me with its siren on, heading into town. It was unusual to see an emergency ambulance in our neighborhood, so I wondered what had happened, but didn't give it much further thought.

When I got back to the house, Miss Bev told me that my younger brother had fallen off the tamarind tree at home and broke his hand; she said the ambulance had taken him to the hospital. I was devastated for my brother Mikel, and started to worried about my other siblings too. I instantly returned to Ken's house to see my other siblings. Although my mother left someone to look after them, I could see the house was dirty and they hardly had any clean clothes. I made a conscious decision in that moment to move back home. Being the eldest daughter, I was used to helping my mother to look after my siblings, especially my last baby sister who was around 3 years old. I knew Ken would continue having his way with me, but I didn't care because by that time I was already used to him. So, I sacrificed myself to be able to look after my brothers and sisters, just like my mother had been sacrificing me all along.

One Last Kiss

Towards the beginning of summer 1999, Ken told me that my mother was doing great in England, and had found a good job and somewhere to live. He also said that she was planning to send for me.

Although I knew this was the plan all along, I was still shocked at how quickly it was happening. I was also shocked that Ken seemed to be on board with the plan. Maybe he thought he was coming to England too. He told me he'd help sort out my passport. He gave me money and instructed me to take some photos after school the next day. I took the pictures and gave them to him. He must have travelled to the central passport office in Montego Bay by himself to apply for my passport, because a couple of weeks after giving him the passport photos, he told me to go to Montego Bay to pick up my passport. I couldn't believe it, but quickly did as he said. I used this opportunity to go to my family's house in Cottage Bottom, as it was near the passport office. I was also missing Mark and wanted to see him, even if it was just for a day. As my mother was away, I felt more flexible to do as I wished in Montego Bay. I was so glad when I laid eyes on Mark – all my emotions for him came rushing back within me. By this time, everyone in our circle knew how we felt about each other, and they kept teasing us, singing silly songs about Mark and I.

"Mya and Mark up in di tree, K I S S I N G!"

I found it cute but annoying; I didn't want the attention to scare him away from me. I told him that my mother was planning to send for me to come to England soon, and showed him my big blue passport. We knew the distance would affect our relationship. I wanted to share an extra special memory with him by giving him a piece of me. I decided to have sex with him at his house. It's key to highlight that although he was my fourth sexual partner by this point (excluding Uncle Bunny), this was the first time I was voluntarily having sex with anyone. But it wasn't what I thought it would be; it was over in a matter of minutes! I felt really awkward afterwards, and went back to Aunt Mavis house, opposite his. I had a shower and came back out later that day but things were awkward between us. Later that evening, I received news that my mother had been trying to get hold of me and I needed to go back home immediately. As it was a bit late for me to travel that evening, I left the next day.

When I got back to Heskit, Ken told me that my mother had bought my plane ticket to leave for England on the 10th August 1999. Luckily for me, the sacrifice I made to leave Bev's house and go back to Ken's didn't last long, because within five months of my mother's departure, I'd joined her in England. I was the first of her six children my mother took from Jamaica.

Escaping Domestic abuse and Child Sexual Abuse

I often ask myself why it took my mother so long to leave such an extremely violent relationship, especially when he was using their relationship to get direct access to sexually abuse me. I often blamed my mother for not meeting or neglecting my essential needs, such as protecting me and keeping me safe. But the truth is, my mother was in such a power-controlled psychological situation that she couldn't even keep her own self safe. She wasn't allowed to be the parent she would have liked to be. There were so many complex reasons as to why it took us so long. The violence impacted my mother's self-belief and self-worth, giving her a thousand tangible reasons why she couldn't leave, such as not having enough money to survive without Ken, or not wanting to uproot her children from our home, school, friends, neighbours, family and community – our roots! My mother also feared that anywhere she went with his children, he would find her and bring them back, which meant she would have to risk her and her children's lives by going back. Although she couldn't see a practical way out beforehand, the longer we stayed in it, the more it caused my mother and I (and other siblings) many deep traumas resulting in anxiety, depression, personality disorders, eating disorders, suicidal thoughts, mental breakdowns, PTSD (Post Traumatic Stress Disorder), abandonment, the constant feeling of being a failure, overwhelmed with fear of immediate and extreme danger, etc.

Domestic abuse is so varied and complex; without proper support, even those with the best intentions end up never leaving at all or keep going back. During the time it took us to escape, my mother suffered greatly! From severe physical abuse to complex psychological abuse and coercive control.

Also, I think it can easily be overlooked just how much a victim tends to lose when escaping violence and abuse. Many people on the outside looking in, tend to focus on what they're likely to ***gain*** from escaping. However, all that is to be gained is not usually promised or tangible, such as: ***a new start without the abuse; change for a better life; standing up for yourself; greater self-esteem and self-confidence; better safety and security; being a better role model for your children; or greater control over your/your children's life and desires.***

However, to fulfill any of these hopes and desires, one may first have to let go of the life they've always known and everything in it. For my mother and her children, this not only meant ***giving up our home, community, family, friends, culture and all our favourite things to do, it also meant giving up our complete roots to travel to a brand new country we'd never been to before***. As exciting as this may seem, there was a lot of risk attached. We left everything behind and only came with the clothes on our back. So many things could've gone wrong. And as you'll see, many things didn't go as planned, but I'm thankful that in the long run, it was the best decision she ever made. To this day, I'm still very grateful that she'd finally escaped with all her children, safely and alive! Looking back now, it's much easier to appreciate that my mother did the best she could with what she had, and for that, I'm eternally grateful.

England

The plane ride was very long, approximately 10 hours, but I was just so excited to be on it, going to London! I'd watched British TV programs, but I never thought I'd be on a British Airways or any other flight going there. The food on the plane was delicious; I couldn't believe that they served rice and peas with chicken, it was like a proper Sunday dinner in Jamaica, except my mother's cooking was much more delicious. I kept picturing what my life was going to be like in England. Reminiscing on some of the houses I'd seen in the TV programs, I thought that when I got to London, I'd live in a huge mansion with a swimming pool in the backyard. I dreamt of how my mother and I would finally have the time to talk over all the bad stuff that Ken had put us through. I couldn't wait to see my mother and to build the relationship I'd always wanted with her. I couldn't wait to feel happy and at ease, without the fear of what could happen next.

I met a girl on the plane called Kim. She was about my age, and was travelling to London to see her family too. We talked all the way along the 10-hour flight, and made promises to keep in touch with each other. When I got off the plane, I was a little bit scared to go through Heathrow airport's security and answer all their questions. My mother had briefed me on the kind of questions they were likely to ask. My greatest fears were, being sent back to the hell hole I came out of in Jamaica or going to prison. I couldn't go back. That would've wasted my mother's money and my opportunity to be free from Ken. I wasn't sure why I was this scared because I hadn't done anything wrong.

A lady escorted me through the airport and reassured me that I'd be with my mother in no time. Walking out of the main part of the airport, I could see a bunch of people holding up all kind of signs that said "Taxi", "Ross"," Billy Jones" etc. The next thing I saw was my mother's face bursting into tears as she laid eyes on me. We had huge smiles on our faces. It was the best feeling being reunited with my mother, away from Ken. We did it!" I thought. It's all over now.

CHAPTER TWO

A New Beginning: Away From The Abuse

Life in England

"Recovering from abuse by someone who was close to you is a long process, and the damage may stay with you and your children for years. You are likely to experience grief, pain and a deep sense of loss: your trust will have been betrayed, your self-esteem and confidence are shattered. In many ways it is like being bereaved – and as with a bereavement, healing will take time." [24]

I've found that many people think once you're physically away from the initial abuse and violence, you should be ok. As my story continues, it will highlight that getting away from the abuse was the first step. The next step was to get support for my deeply complex needs.

At the airport, one of my cousins, Faith stepped forward to claim me from the airport staff who'd escorted me from the plane. My mother didn't have the necessary paperwork and so it was arranged for my cousin Faith to legally receive me. We collected my bags and

24 https://www.womensaid.org.uk/the-survivors-handbook/surviving-after-abuse/

went to her car. Being the capital, I felt that London was nothing compared to what was sold to us in Jamaica. I couldn't believe the condition of some of the houses we drove past coming from the airport, or the potholes in the road. I remember seeing the crowded areas and hoping that we were going somewhere less crowded and more luxurious with a swimming pool round the back, like it was portrayed on the television in Jamaica. When we reached Aunt Pam's block in Brixton, I was disappointed at the exterior. Looking at the rubbish on the ground, the place didn't look very welcoming, plus it was clear there was no pool in sight.

It was a tall building with an outside staircase that leads up to each flat. The building seemed to have many other flats which all looked the same, but differentiated by allocated door numbers. This was unlike the houses in Jamaica, where everyone made their house look unique according to their own likeness, style and affordability. I looked around me and saw a few more buildings that looked the same as ours. I couldn't understand why everyone built their houses the same as everyone else's in the community. I thought I'd definitely get lost if I went out by myself!

When we got into the flat, my first impression was that it looked much better inside than outside; it was clean and nicely decorated. It reminded me of how we decorated our homes in Jamaica – the only thing was that the flat was much smaller than our houses back home, especially Mama's house where Aunt Pam lived before, she travelled to England. Although I was very happy to be there, I was still in shock over not being in the mansion I had dreamt about. Aunt Pam greeted me with lots of joy, laughter and happiness. I was one of her favourite (grand) nieces and so she was ever so happy to see that I had finally made it to England. Some of my other cousins came to greet me too, such as her two daughters Ann and Winnie. I didn't share my mixed emotions with anyone because I didn't want them to think I was being ungrateful, so I just kept a smile on my face all day.

The day I arrived felt like a huge celebration with my family. Everyone was being so friendly, even an elderly neighbour of Aunt Pam's called Norris. My mother had told me not to bring any clothes from Jamaica, so the same day I arrived she took me shopping in Brixton. I could tell she hadn't thought this through properly. Although she meant well and wanted me to have nice, new clothes (unlike some of the old rags back home), she perhaps didn't have the kind of money required to buy me all the necessities I needed. I recall saying I should've brought some of my clothes so that she didn't have to buy everything new for me.

Whilst we were out in Brixton, I remember seeing many fast food shops and got really excited about how easily accessible they were compared to back home. One of my favorite places to eat was Morley's on Brixton Road (in front of the police station). I loved their fried chicken, burgers and chips and most of all, their BBQ spare ribs. It was so delicious; I couldn't have enough! In Jamaica we'd rarely eat out. When we did, we'd go to KFC as a luxury and as delicious as KFC was, they didn't serve BBQ spare ribs. So, this was definitely one good improvement for me in London. Looking back now, all that meat isn't good for the mind, body or spiritual growth but I didn't know any better at the time, plus it was cheap and convenient so I gladly ate as much as I could.

Unresolved deep-rooted Pain

On the day of my arrival, my mother told me I'd be staying with Aunt Pam to help out with babysitting Winne's son until she found a bigger place for us to live together. I loved Aunt Pam very much and generally this wouldn't have been a problem, however this wasn't what I expected; I had been looking forward to having my mother all to myself for the first time, and working through our past challenges.

There was so much I wanted to tell her about the horrible things that had happened to me. I wanted my mother to tell me she was sorry for my pain and hug me tightly to let me know it's over now. I wanted her to promise me that things would be different moving forward. I wanted to be able to trust my mother and relieve myself of the burden I'd been carrying for so long. I wanted so badly to believe that Ken was the main reason affecting the bond I so desperately desired to have with my mother; now that he was out of the way, there was nothing stopping us.

Deep down I knew my mother wasn't a bad woman; I knew she loved me, especially as she worked three cleaning jobs tirelessly each day to raise the money to bring me first from Jamaica. I knew she did this to remove me from the abusive situation I was in as quickly as she could. I knew that she could've easily taken my other siblings for good reason too. But knowing something and feeling it is two different things. I wanted so badly to ***feel*** loved by her. This could easily have been achieved if we had spent quality time together, just me and her, talking over past events and creating a better foundation for our future. We could've settled the dust, cried together and held each other tight. She could've told me how she really felt inside. It mattered to me to know these things to help create that mutual basis with her. But this desire was never fulfilled. My mother was so busy with her three cleaning jobs (one early morning and one day shift at Sita; and one evening job at Channel 4), seven days per week. She did this in order to survive and bring me from Jamaica so quickly. She continued to do this so she could take the rest of her children from Ken.

At the time I didn't appreciate her determination, hardwork and commitment to her other five children. All I could think about were my own needs. On one hand my mother was my superhero. On the other hand, I continued to blame her for most, if not all of my pain. I knew that if we'd focused on reducing the gap between us, it would've gone a long way to mending these two extreme perceptions I had of her. Although I was away from the physical violence and abuse, I continued to live in confusion, hurt and pain each day, mainly caused by neglect of my needs as well as mental and emotional abuse.

Racism

I had no support for the deep-root and extreme trauma I'd experienced in Jamaica. I had no support to help me adjust into the new life I was living in London. I found everything here so different to Jamaica, from the culture and language to the people and expectations of me. It was like I was living an endless out of body experience. I'd even experienced racism and didn't realize what it was at the time, or how to articulate it. It just felt really uncomfortable, dismissive and disrespected which reinforced my negative perception about myself. For example, an old white man put his hands out in front of me to stop me entering a 109 bus in Brixton, so that the white lady with her baby and everyone else could enter first. Out of respect for the old man I stood there silently in my discomfort and waited until he removed his hand and allowed me on. By then the bus was really packed so I had to stand downstairs with some of the other passengers holding on tightly as the bus started moving. It was so uncomfortable standing there with everyone staring at me.

All the excitement of coming to England soon wore off, and I found myself missing Jamaica like crazy, especially Mark. I asked my mother for a calling card so I could call my friends to let them know I'd reached England safely. When my mother eventually got me the card, I called Mark first. Initially I didn't get through to him but I continued calling until he finally answered. I thought he'd be so excited to hear from me which he probably was, but it didn't come across in his voice. In fact, he seemed distant and not bothered to hear from me. I thought he'd found out about Ken but I dared not ask him.

In hindsight, maybe he felt just as uncomfortable as I did speaking to him over the phone for the first time and knowing there's so much distance between us. Maybe he was upset that I'd left straight after we had sex for the first time. I guess there was a lot of pressure on our relationship. We struggled to build conversations which made it even more awkward. Our conversations were brief and scanty until one of us released the other by creating some reason as to why we had to go. I tried calling him a few more times again but the connection was never the same over the phone, so I stopped calling and just believed he didn't love me anymore. I'm not aware that he tried to call me. I did question myself whether he used me for sex but deep down, I always knew it was more than that. At the time, I blamed coming to England for ruining one of the best things in my life!

Settling In

After a short while at Aunt Pam's, I stayed at my cousin's Ann and Faith's house in Tulse Hill. They both had children which I helped to look after.

By December 1999, I started Stockwell Park High School in year 9. I was now living with my mother in Brixton Hill along with my sister Joy who'd just came from Jamaica. A few months later, my mother sent for my big brother James and my two baby sisters Sheridan and Kayla; shortly after that, she sent for my brother Mikel. We were all here in England together now, but everything seemed so busy.

My mother had a new partner, Mick. Between him and her three jobs, she was hardly ever at home. She often left me in charge of the chores, to look after the house and cook dinner. I went from not being allowed in the kitchen in Jamaica as I wasn't "old enough", to cooking full meals for my siblings in England with no cooking lessons or instructions, just my own intuition. One day I put ketchup in a pot of curry chicken, thinking ketchup could go into anything, but oh no, it had its limits – I got such a beating from my mother that day, I've never put ketchup in curry ever again!

Stockwell Park High School

I remember feeling sad most of the time. At home I had so much responsibility whilst still getting harsh beatings. I was also being controlled by deep-unresolved and unaddressed past traumatic issues. At school, the kids would laugh at my "big thighs" and called me names like "kebab legs". They also got me to say certain words in Jamaican accent then mocked me when I did. This included swear words such as "bombo clart" or "pussy clart!"

I wanted to feel like one of them because then I could hide behind their shadow without the spotlight being on me. They made me feel so different. I didn't get their jokes. I didn't get the culture. I didn't speak like them. I had little or no knowledge of the TV shows and programs they talked about all the time. I couldn't share my past in the same fun way that they seemed familiar with. I sat, listened and laughed for the most of it. In fact, I loved my education and wanted to learn, which was another thing that made me stand out from the rest. They talked a lot in class, did very little work and disrespected the teachers when challenged about their behaviour or work. Unlike me, they also seemed not too bothered about punishment such as getting sent out of class or having their parents contacted by the school. I knew that if the school had to contact my mother about my behaviour, I'd be a dead child! So school was very intense, I didn't know what was the right thing to do. I desperately wanted to fit in, but I didn't like how they treated me. I also didn't want to risk my education or get into trouble just to fit in. I was torn. But at the same time, I knew that I had to prove myself if they were ever going to accept me as one of them. My aim was to act a bit like them, but never get caught.

One day at school we were told that the Spanish teacher had suddenly left, and we'd be replacing Spanish with French class until they found a replacement Spanish teacher. I was gutted! I loved Spanish and didn't know or have any interest in learning French. That day in class, I wasn't in the mood to do any work and didn't care when the teacher tried to challenge me. To make my life easier, I told the teacher I had a headache. He told me to sit quietly and rest my head on the table. As soon as he turned his back, I started chatting away and making fun of the teacher. I didn't see when he came up behind me; all I felt was an unexpected hand on my shoulder – I automatically reacted by turning around and punching the person in their face. It was the teacher and he was very shocked! His eyes bulged out of his head in disbelief of what had just happened. He stormed out of the class to get the Head Teacher, Miss Tapper. I panicked and quickly made up a story that he punched me first. To my surprise, the entire class said they saw when the teacher "hit me first" and this is what they told the Miss Tapper when she came to speak to the class. I never saw that French teacher ever again. At the time this happened, I was happy because it gave me a way to actually make new friends whilst not getting into trouble with my mother. I thought it worked out perfectly, without giving a second thought about the French teacher or his family. In hindsight I'm truly sorry for what I did. I hope he escaped any serious consequences and found another job with as much ease as possible.

I couldn't believe how easy it was to play the game; after that little taste of rebellion I wanted more, but I knew I still had to be careful in case my mother found out. I soon became the bully that was bullied – mocking the quieter children that were there for me when no-one else was. Deep down I actually preferred the quieter children such as Isabella and Caitlin because they liked doing their work, but I didn't like being around them when the bullies were around; I thought they made me look bad. I blamed them for getting picked on because they were used to it, I wasn't. So, to survive, I knew I had to be on the stronger team. I acted up a lot in order to please my new friends, including leaving school at lunchtime to smoke cigarettes in the local estate blocks. I was hot tempered too, and always up for a good fight – that's one of the things that didn't change in me from when I was at school in Jamaica. Then one day after my sister Joy had joined me at Stockwell Park, we got into the biggest fight that led to my sister and I getting expelled from school for two weeks, whilst the girl whom we fought spent a week in the hospital. All because the girl said to Joy: "Your mum!" This statement was enough back then to anger anyone including Joy, myself and the rest of the school children that joined in the fight to beat up the girl. Our mother was called to the school to pick us up, and I could tell from the look in my mother's eyes that I was going to get it when we got home. No amount of lies or pleading could save us from what was waiting. In addition to the beatings, we were grounded and given more chores at home that kept us busy throughout the two weeks. I couldn't wait to go back to school and see my friends again.

Generally, I found school here to be so different from the schools in Jamaica, mainly because the work was less challenging and we could use a calculator in class! It became less engaging and I soon loss interest. I remember Mr. Chambers was my favorite teacher - he taught me Media Studies which I wasn't really interested in, but I liked his class. I was more interested in my friends and their ways of life. They were fun! They were my new distraction! They influenced me to move the goal post and put it wherever I wanted. I was great at following them although deep down I knew better than this. At this time my mother worked at night shifts at Macdonald's in Brixton Hill. When she went to work, I'd sneak out to meet my friends Melanie, Chantelle, Adelle, Danny and others. Danny seemed to be the ringleader and I liked his "rude boy" approach and loved hanging out with him. We'd jumped the school wall and found a place to chill where we smoked weed and drank alcohol, play music, amongst other things. I often witness them robbed people on the street and it intrigued me how organized and committed they were. Their lifestyles looked so much cooler than mine and they seemed to have much more freedom too.

Mick: Re-victimisation

My mother's boyfriend Mick moved in. He was a tall darkskinned man from Kingston, Jamaica with braces and dimples, a few years younger than my mother. He got on well with us until he started hitting my mother in the house and on the street. I hated the way my mother was so into him. I couldn't understand how you could love someone that treated you like that. Of course, it was easy for me to judge as I wasn't the one in the situation. But I think it triggered my own unresolved childhood issues, and I saw Mick as a similar perpetrator to Ken. I saw the same hurt and pain in my mother's eyes. I heard the same blows, screams and saw the busted and swollen lips and eyes afterwards. I knew I could never allow him to touch me, and just hoped he never tried.

I think my mother wanted to please Mick so bad that she fell pregnant for him as he didn't have any children of his own. She must have thought a child would make him a better person. But I was very disappointed! All along I was holding onto some hope that my mother would find the strength to get him to leave, but now that she was pregnant, he wasn't going anywhere. He was to be in our lives forever! I hated my mother for adding to my existing burden without even helping me to unload existing baggage. Although my mother lost the baby (probably through domestic violence), she soon got pregnant for him again and gave birth to my second to last brother – MJ. At first, I didn't bond well with MJ, not like my other siblings. It was mostly left to Joy to help our mother looked after him.

By this time, I'd lost so much interest at home and became even more rebellious. I started coming home from school much later than usual, then I'd make up lies about why I was late. Sometimes I'd feel like my mother would beat me because of the ridiculous nature of the lie. For example, I'd tell her that I was an hour late home because of traffic, or due to the bus drivers changing shifts. I started smoking more and drinking too. I enjoyed spending time with my school friend and getting up to mischief much more than I wanted to be home. After school we'd go in the local corner shops and steal snacks or we'd rob anyone we see and use the money to buy chicken and chips. But then my mother changed the rules on me. She said as it took me 30 minutes to get to school in the mornings, I should be home within 30 minutes after school. At first, I thought this was ridiculous as I'd be the only child breaking my neck to get home after school which wouldn't look too great for my street creds, but I decided to play her game. I'd rush home after school, change my clothes, wait for her to go to her cleaning night job, then I'd go back out to meet my friends. My friends were my family as they made me feel belonged and wanted. They seemed to enjoy my company and gave me their attention. I knew most of what I was doing was wrong but I didn't care – as no-one else seemed to.

At this time, we'd get up to all kind of things such as street robbery and fighting people in the streets in groups; and breaking into our school at nights. As long as I got back home before my mother she'd never know, as none of my siblings never say a word. I'm not sure if my neighbours were even aware of what I was up to and I definitely didn't miss the community spirit we had in Jamaica as everyone here minded their own business.

Mick Hit Me!

Then one day after school, I was looking through some pictures in my mother's room (which was unusual as I'd stay out of her room since Mick moved in). I must have said something "out of place" when he suddenly punched me in the face – I couldn't believe what had just happened! I thought "That's it, your days are over now!" My mother didn't really do anything about it. I thought she could choose not to do anything when he hits her, but I'm not her. I thought either the men in our family will devour him now, or the police will. Either way, he'd never come back to our house. I called some of my big cousins including Redz and Vinnie and told them what had happened. They all seemed very concerned for me, yet hesitant to do anything about it. One of them even told me that my mother made them promise not to get involved in her life, and they didn't want to break their promise. I was speechless! I couldn't believe she'd done that. Surely, she didn't like the way those men treated her, so why would she hold off protection? Nevertheless, I tried to convince my cousins that their promise with my mother didn't concern me, but they didn't agree and so didn't do anything about it.

In an absolute rage I called the police and reported what Mick had done to me. The police came. They spoke to my mother and took her report, then told me there's nothing they can do based on my mother's testimony. They said my mother told them that she was in the room with Mick and I (which she was) but she didn't see him hit me??!!!! My instant thought was "She lied to protect him over me!" Because she was my legal guardian, at the time, the law required her cooperation to press charges. I was now out of options and there was nothing the police or I could do. Yet again, there would be no justice. I just had to put up with the situation no matter how hard it was. My mother had disappointed me again, deeply.

A part of me believed she was intentionally trying to hurt me. Yet all I ever wanted was for her to let me see her standing up for me and putting me first. It was too much to deal with. Even thinking about it now still brings back some of those painful emotions. I kept thinking about how nothing had changed, and even though we'd left Jamaica, away from the initial violence and abuse, we were still suffering as if we hadn't.

So, although the environment was different, we were still the same people reacting to circumstances in the same way. No healing hadn't taken place as a result of coming away from the abuse and violence, and therefore there was no change to our behaviour. Our power waas robbed from us in Jamaica and here stuck in our learnt behaviours and freely giving it up.

I couldn't understand why my mother was putting me through this nightmare again, unless this was her intention, but I couldn't imagine what I'd done to deserve it. I knew she was scared of Mick but I believed the police would've put him away if she'd told them everything, especially about the fact he had no legal right to reside in the UK (we were waiting to hear back from the Home Office about our application to stay in the UK, but Mick didn't have a valid application at all). This was her opportunity as well as mine to get out before something worse happened, but in my opinion at the time, she chose to stay with him.

As a practitioner who now supports women and girl survivors of abuse and violence to rebuild their lives, I can understand that it wasn't as easy as I had thought, to break away from an abuser. I've recognised that my child-self blamed my mother a lot for everything that happened to her. "As my mother, she was meant to protect me from all the violence and abuse. She's meant to know what my needs are and fulfill them. She meant to be there for me when I needed her." These were just some of the thoughts that have replayed in my mind over and over again. But that's because my wounded child-self didn't know any better. She didn't understand abuse/violence and how it impacts its victims, nor didn't she understand how my mother's own lived experiences may've affected her, long before I came in the picture. This is what many people do, they blame the victim when it was NEVER their fault.

Furthermore, even if the police had arrested Mick, there was no guarantee he would've been sent to prison or deported back to Jamaica, so the fear of angering him in this way could've proven deadly for any one of us. Of course, as a child I wasn't thinking about this either and to be fair, I shouldn't have had to. I needed love, care and protection from my care givers – my mother trusted Mick to be a responsible person around her children and he broke all of our trust. As my mother was stuck again in another domestic abuse relationship, she was unable to give me what I needed, so I kept suffering.

Rebel with a cause

Seeking attention, I became even more rebellious and got involved in all kind of things, including spending more time with my school friends outside of school and taking greater risks. The greater the risk, the more alive I felt inside. These risk became another form of temporary fix along with drugs, alcohol, sex, partying, shop-lifting, street robbery, fighting, etc. Amongst my school friends, all of us had some kind of disturbed childhood, and none of us were getting the help we needed. This made me feel more at home with this group friends. We felt well justified not giving a damn about anything or anyone!

Mikel soon got into trouble of his own will with the police and wasn't around us anymore, leaving my mother to look after his son. Our 2-bedroom flat in Brixton Hill got really crowded with Aunt Patsy who came from Jamaica and was living with us as well as another one of our cousin Von was also living there with his family. I fell for one of Von's stepson Kemal, and Joy liked the other brother. We often locked ourselves in the bathroom kissing, but we wouldn't dare do anymore out of fear of being caught. Soon, we were all getting evicted; Kemal and I planned to have sex for the first time on our last day in the house.

On the last day, we did have sex, but got caught by my mother. This was exactly what we thought was the worst-case scenario and it was playing out right in front of our eyes. Kemal jumped through the window. I opened the door to let my mother in, pretending like nothing's wrong. I tried lying to her face until she showed me my trousers was inside out! Needless to say, I got some good beaten that evening.

We spent about five months living in a one bedroom in Stockwell – less than five minutes' walk from my school. The younger children slept on the bed whilst my mother and her older slept on the floor. We then moved to a bigger property in West Norwood.

'Seeing my mother struggling to look after herself and 7 children on her own, I didn't want to burden her by asking for things I knew she couldn't afford such as a new pair of Nike trainers or certain name brand clothes. My friends had all the latest clothing and they introduced me to stealing from the shops. At first I was scared at the thought of being caught but after escaping the first time with new underwears, I was happy to try again. I loved the thrill it gave me inside. The stuff we stole felt like added bonus. But sometimes I'd get caught and the police called although in the end, that didn't stop me. On one occasion I took my two baby sisters for a "day out" in central London and ended up getting caught for shoplifting. I was put in the back of the police car with my two sisters next to me. I thought my mother was literally going to kill me but the police let me go and told me to go straight home with my sisters. On our way home, I bribed my sisters not to tell our mother anything and they didn't.

Social Service

The more issues I had at home, the more I'd go out and rebel with my friends. When I got caught, I'd get some serious battering from my mother, which that made me hated her even more, if that was even possible. Although I hated the beatings, I thought they were as normal here as they were in Jamaica until I found out I was the only one amongst my friends still getting beating and so I thought this was another way my mother was showing she didn't like her me.

One night after getting arrested for attempted street robbery, the police went to search my house for any other stolen goods. Although they wouldn't have found anything there, the impact of a police search of our house was extremely emotional for my mother and my siblings. I spent that night at the police station but was bailed out the next day. My mother was waiting for me with all that built up anger, and when I got through the door, the way she grabbed me and started beating the life out of me! The next morning, I had school, but I was in so much pain and could hardly sit down properly. I was so angry and wanted it all to be over, but I wasn't sure how. When I got to school, one of the teachers noticed the difference in my usual bubbly and talkative character. As soon as she asked me what happened, I started to tell her how my mother beats me all the time. I told her she didn't have to take my word for it, she could ask my sister Joy.

When they spoke to Joy seperately, apparently Joy collaborated my story. They got Social Services involved immediately. Although there was a part of me that was still a little scared of what my mother would do or say, I was mostly relieved and overjoyed thinking the beatings would have to stop.

Furthermore, I didn't even want to live with my mother anymore. I'd convinced myself that she wasn't my mother and that explained all the horrible treatment I'd suffered at her hands – or the hands of her partners – and why she didn't do anything about it at the time. I was ready to be placed in a new and loving home where people would talk to me about how I was feeling and offer me the necessary (emotional and mental) support I needed. There was also a small part of me that expected my mother to get into trouble and that part of me was happy – it may be the only justice I'd ever get.

The Social Services met with me at my school, and I answered all of their questions. They explained that they would meet with Joy and then my mother too. After which they would decide on the right course of action. Going home that day, I felt untouchable. I knew my mother couldn't hit me again I waited in anticipation for the outcome of the case, and was even dreaming about what my new family would be like. To my dismay they didn't remove me from my home. Instead, they became empathetic towards my mother's situation and wanted to release her from some of the burden she was carrying in exchange that she treat her children better. They explained that as a single parent, my mother was under a lot of stress working three jobs, looking after seven children and trying hard to keep up with private rent. So, they gave us new home, and regular financial support in exchange for no more beatings from her.

Writing about this, I'm now so thankful for the help from the social workers at Olive Morris House in Lambeth although at the time, I took this to be another disappointing news that was against me. I wanted to leave my mother's house and nothing less wouldn't suffice. I thought my mother was so good at pretending that she even fool the damn social workers! I was absolutely gutted! Nevertheless, the support they gave my mother meant she didn't have to keep working three jobs. We were provided with a new and spacious home in Tulse Hill as well as monthly financial support. I believe my mother even got support filling an application at the Home Office. I wish I could've seen how this was the right thing for us at the time. Instead, I rebelled even more because I didn't feel like they acted in my best interest, as no one ever did. I thought they just liked my mother and was doing it for her. Eventually I found consolation was that my mother couldn't touch me anymore. So, I started to walk in and out of the house whenever I liked without showing any respect for her.

Misfits

By this point, I'd just met a cousin of mine for the first-time, and we instantly became very good friends. We called her 'Cherina'.

Cherina had a disturbed upbringing that made me feel more empathetic towards her than anyone else I'd ever met. I developed a soft spot for her and felt the need to protect her. Cherina lived in walking distance from me in West Norwood. We started spending a lot of time together with her group of friends who also became my friends. We were all around the same age, but they went to a different Secondary school. As before, this group were attracted to each other because of our pain from unresolved childhood issues. I could tell that these girls were more than just friends, they were family, and I was glad to be a part of their bond. To this day I'm still very close to Cherina and Sarah. There were five of us in the group, including myself. One of the girls I no longer talk to, another one I hardly see, and the final one has since been murdered by her baby father a few years ago.

We passed time doing similar things as I did with my group of school friends, except now we also did bupsing, binged eat a lot and much more street robbery. Bupsing was kind of new to me. For us, it was basically the skillful art of getting a man to give us what we wanted without giving him anything he wanted.

For example, they'd give us food, clothes, trainers, cannabis, alcohol and money. But we never gave them any sexual attention which is what they wanted. As most of us didn't have any source of income and didn't get regular money from our parents, this became our main source of generating money, along with street robbery.

Violence was commonly used in street robbery as a way of getting our victims' bags away from them and into our possession. One kick from me and they'd either drop to the ground or they'd hand over their bags. Either way, it was much easier for them to "coorporate" rather than "exasperate" the situation, knowing they were outnumbered. These crimes were mostly perpetrated at nights against lonely women and girls. We found it to be very powerful and profitable. Not only would we find cash in their purses, we'd also sold their valuables to the highest bidder such as their phones, passport and bank cards. Being broken ourselves, this was yet another temporary fix than kept us going.

One day we were bored and passing time looking through the window out on the road at Cherina's flat in West Norwood. We saw a group of girls walking down the road. As they walked pass our building, we shouted "Crankaay", "Beyonkaa", and "Tidle wave". For us these were silly words we created that made us laugh for no reason. For the other girls, we were disrespecting them, and they wouldn't have it. Unbeknown to us, they went and got the rest of their "gang", came back in their numbers and pushed their way into Cherina's flat. I was terrified. I'd never seen anything like this before! I was scared and glad they didn't come for me. Instead they attacked Cherina and beat her up severely. Although Cherina was slightly older than all of us, she was the smallest in size and so she was often the victim of attacks. I watched helplessly as they trampled my cousin. There were only four of us compare to so many of them, they couldn't all fit in the room. Plus, they had both boys and girls in their group – and were of all different sizes. I wanted so much to protect her but I was scared for my life. I didn't want them to turn on me. Initially after they left, I felt a huge sense of relief then I got really angry as I was beating up myself inside with thoughts like, "how could you have...?" What a waste you are." You're not as bad as you thought you were. In fact, you're a "scaredy cat!". We made a few phone calls to get help from some family/friends in Brixton. In no time, our 'back up' came and we went to hunt down the main girls that beat up Cherina. Eventually we found a couple of them and we beat them up on the street. I remember I had to go home straight afterwards as I had a tag on my right foot and I didn't want to break my curfew and have it trigger the police to my house.

Although we got our revenge that night, it didn't stop there. This battle went on for years until one night, my life flashed in front of me! Before I go into that, let me catch up on the rest of the story.

Crime Watch

We had everything we wanted; from the latest clothes, trainers, mobile phones, drugs and alcohol, to buying two to three meals per day each and still having money in our pockets. Back then it was just as important to us having the last trainers and phone as it was to eat regularly each day.

We felt we were doing pretty good for ourselves, until one day we were told by another family member that we appeared on Crime Watch. I still don't know how true this was but I certainly believed it at the time, and so did a lot of other family members. Cherina and I officially became the black sheep of the family bringing shame and disgrace upon the "saints" which were our family. We weren't invited to many family events and when we turned up uninvited, we were frowned upon.

Sexual Health

"Adult childhood sexual abuse survivors disproportionately use health care services and incur greater health care costs compared with adults who did not experience abuse" This is because they are likely to have more sexual partners and are less skilled at protecting themselves." [25]

25 https://m.acog.org/Clinical-Guidance-and-Publications/Committee-Opinions/Committee-on-Health-Care-for-Underserved-Women/Adult-Manifestations-of-Childhood-Sexual-Abuse

We were sexually active with multiple sexual partners and we didn't always use protection. We often visited Brooks in Brixton and/ or the Sexual Health Clinic in Camberwell. We took regular tests for pregnancy and sexually transmitted diseases. I'm so thankful that I never got pregnant back then, or caught any life-changing sexual infections or diseases.

Coming from a childhood of uncontrollable sexual desires to becoming an overly sexualise teen with daddy issues, when it came to men, sex was all I knew. I didn't realize I was looking for a 'daddy figure' in these sexual relationships, which was even more twisted considering my main perpetrator was my step-dad – a man I thought of as my dad.

Needless to say, I had many unhealthy and toxic relationships with men, which I now recognise was a result of my years of childhood sexual abuse and rape. I knew nothing about self-value or self-worth at the time. In fact, I knew nothing about my inner self! If I really liked a guy, I expected him to like me back. I knew I had a pretty face, lovely smile, desirable body and I'd learnt how to use my "assets" to my sexual advantage. If he didn't like me back, I'd offer him sex to make him want me. But of course, after he got what he wanted, oftentimes, there was no hanging around; if he did, it was mostly to get more of the same.

This would make me feel even worse about myself and I knew I had no-one to blame but me. I prefer older men and found boys my age or younger to be immature; they automatically fell below my standards, and so, they wouldn't stand a chance with me.

I also loved different sexual adventures which I found empowering at the time. From toys to mixed gender, sexual games became very fun with little or no boundaries amongst certain groups of friends.

In my late teens, I did my first smear test to check the health of my cervix, although it wasn't generally advisable before 25 years old, because the body was still developing. My test came back abnormal. This was worrying to me for many reasons including the fact I knew I wanted children. It resulted in frequent and uncomfortable visits to the colposcopy clinic where they examined my cervix and vagina area with a colposcope. They also performed painful biopsy procedures. I now know they were checking for things like cancer, but at the time, I was scared and overwhelmed with the pain which brought back triggering memories from my past. In the end, I stopped attending. I've since had a handsome and strong son and I'm grateful to be fit and healthy today.

Another issue I had in this area was very painful period every month, to the point that it affected my day to day activities such as going to school or work. Each month at the same time, I'd be wrapped up in bed and drugged up on lots of painkillers. This carried on until I went on the Depo Injection contraception in my late teens which stopped my period. For years I remained on it even when I wasn't sexually active. This was because of the relieved it gave me from not having my usual painful periods. I'm now so pleased to say I've healed myself in this area through my alternative practices. I now allow my usual monthly flow – completely painfree.

Kay: A Bupse or Angel in Disguise?

In my final year of school, I met an older guy called Kay. Seeing as I was so materialistic and attracted to older men, he was the perfect guy for me. He flaunted his wealth by driving three expensive cars, wore expensive jewellery and clothes. The only thing was I found him to be very ugly. Although I wasn't physically attracted to him at first, one of the reasons I stuck around is because he seemed genuinely kind and different from the other guys.

I'm glad I stuck with him because he was there for me when I needed support. For example, he gave me money and paid for all the things I needed for my school graduation. I was graduating from Stockwell Park High School with no GCSE's, yet that didn't seem to bother me on the surface. At least I'd bothered to turn up to my exams, even if I was drunk, high and tired most of the time. Some of my friends didn't sit their exams at all! Deep down I knew I was capable of more but I was so lost, I had no idea how to find my way. I let down my mother and teachers, including Mr Chambers from Media Studies, who clearly wanted better for me. All I cared about was dressing up and looking beautiful on my Graduation Day. I'd seen so many films about proms and graduation and wanted to feel special like the other children.

My mother and I had another fall-out, so I couldn't turn to her to get money for the things I needed. Besides, by this point I was acting like a "proper grown woman" and so the saying in Jamaica is that, "if yuh ah big woman, gwan guh get wah yuh want!"

Kay was the only one I could've relied on financially. He gave me plenty of money which I used to buy my dress, get my hair, nails and eyelashes done; and everything else I needed to look and feel beautiful on that day. It was so lovely seeing all my school friends all dressed up in their best clothes. The boys wore suit and ties whilst the girls wore gowns and make-up. We took lots of pictures! It was clear to me that I was one of the most beautiful of them all. After the ceremony, Kay surprised me in a white limousine and took me for a celebratory dinner with a few of my family and friends, including Joy and Aunty Patsy. It was my first time in a limo and I felt so special. After that day, everyone around me who knew about Kay loved and respected him, regardless of his age, including my mother and Aunt Patsy – they could see his intentions were genuine.

Gap Year: The Street Life

I took a gap year after school because I had no sense of direction of what I wanted to do. By this time, my life heavily revolved around my friends, including Cherina, Sarah and Ash. We spent most days and nights hanging out together. From the moment we woke up we would be on the phone to each other planning our day together. I attempted to do an evening course at Croydon college but after a couple of weeks I dropped out. I felt I was missing out on too much fun with my friends. By this time, Cherina had been placed in temporary Council accommodation in Peckham. I chose to spend so much of my time at her house, that I stopped going back home for a while; it was probably around six months that I didn't go home or contact my mother. I was able to survive mainly off bupsing men and street robbery to get money to fulfil all my basic needs including clothes, food, cannabis and alcohol. I can remember Sarah telling me on many occasions how easy busping seemed to me. She used to say "All you do is smile and bat your eyelashes then they (the men) give you anything you want!" I didn't realize I'd become the "Bupsing Queen". However, I was definitely confident in my abilities to play this game, and I knew how to play it to my advantage. I gained pleasure out of outsmarting some of these grown-ass men who were looking for sexual favours, when I was barely 16 years old. Besides, it was one of the few times I was utilizing my natural intelligence to get what I want without any form of violence.

But no matter how good you are at these things, someone else is always better. I say that because one of my bupse took me shopping in Central London. I bought everything I wanted including clothes, shoes, handbags, jewellery and underwear. I had many bags in his car. Before he dropped me off, we sat in his car talking. I wanted to leave but I didn't want him to suspect that I was using him and take back the shopping. He wanted sex. Usually I'd say no and find a way out of the situation but on this occasion, I went along with his request. I lay there on his car seat as he took what he wanted. Afterwards, he kicked me out on the streets and threw my handbag at me. Allowing him to get his way backfired on me and I lost everything he'd bought. I was so disgusted with myself and I haven't told anyone before disclosing it here.

Peckham Beef

I had many different experiences during this time. On several occasions I was offered lots of money to sell serious drugs such as crack/cocaine but I declined. I was offered money to transport these drugs across the UK using hotels and B&Bs, but I declined. The most I did was to sell British passports and credit cards, but that was a way of getting rid of valuables left over from street-robbery. I also watched as they transformed passports from one identity into another. There were more risks involved in this lifestyle of drugs, sex and crime than I'd ever imagined!

We had many "mandem" friends in Peckham. Unbeknown to us, we'd developed enemies from the local girls' "gang". They were after us because they'd heard we were from Brixton. At the time, "***Brikies***" (people from Brixton) weren't allowed in "***Pecknaam***" (Peckham). I didn't really get this area code war but I had to at least be aware of it. To this day, area code, now postcode war is responsible for so many deaths and serious injuries of young people, especially those from the black community. Just by us being in Peckham was enough to get attacked. They tried to beat us up a number of times near Cherina's house, which was in the center of Peckham, near the Library. They also tried to attack us on Old Kent Road outside of a nightclub. I never backed down from a good fight, but I'm not stupid enough to fight a group of girls throwing broken bottles after us. They also shouted, "Go back to Brixton!" It felt like trouble always followed us wherever we went. Thankfully, our mandem friends protected us from this point. Some of these boys were like our brothers and some were our boyfriends. They showed us we could count on them in case of anything. We became much more open around them and often chilled together in Cherina's flat.

At some point later, I had a fight with one of the younger boys who surprisingly beat me up and I saw how their loyalties shifted. Eventually it became obvious they didn't owe us anything.

Returning Home

One morning, one of my friends shouted out to me that my mother was approaching Cherina's flat. I was so shocked! How did she find me, and why was she here? In that moment I went from being a "big woman" surviving on her own to being that scared little girl again. As my mother walked up the stairs and stood there looking around the flat, I instantly felt her disgust and disappointment which was evident by the look on her face. Without her even saying a word, I became aware of my surroundings; dirty food containers all over the floor, dirty plates packed in the kitchen sink, clothes all over the place, and worst of all, the boys who were sleeping in the flat.

My mother started shouting at me to get up because she'd come for me. She said "Mi ah send yuh guh back ah Jamaica cause mi ave enuf ah yuh!" I'd heard stories of other African-Caribbean parents who sent their children to their homeland because they were finding it too challenging to raise them in the UK. I knew she didn't stand a chance trying to send me back to Jamaica; she had more chance of doing that when I first came to the UK and was disappointed with what I'd seen! However, I didn't want the shouting and embarrassment in front of my friends, as it didn't look good for my "tamzkid" status or street creds. So, I obediently went with my mother and she took me home.

By this time, we'd moved from West Norwood and were living in a 4-5 bedroom ground floor flat in Tulse Hill Estate near Brixton. I remember returning home and there was no more talk of sending me back to Jamaica. Instead, there were some new terms and conditions, most of which I was happy with, such as the fact that I had my own room for the first time! I could finally have my own space. I was allowed to see my friends and have them over to visit me. It was also clear that my mother wasn't allowed to hit me (or any of my brothers or sisters). But what I struggled with was my mother's curfew required me to be home by 9pm each night. Considering my night time lifestyle, as well as the freedom I'd had at Cherina's house, I couldn't understand the need for this huge restriction and inconvenience on my life. I was willing to stay home all day if it meant I could go out at night and stay out later – but my mother wouldn't budge on the 9pm curfew which became the main cause for further conflicts.

The Cycle Continues: Domestic Violence

My mother soon married a man named George who I thought would help to bring peace and love in our lives, but then he started beating her like all her other partners before.

I remember giving up on any agreement with her, and decided to do what I wanted because she clearly was doing the same. On day

I stayed home in my room all day, then started getting ready around 7pm. By 8pm I was ready to leave the house, but my mother had locked the door with the key; she thought it was too late to leave the house and was convinced I wouldn't be back in time for my curfew. Rebelling against this, I jumped straight through the window and went about my business, not caring about the consequences. A part of me felt like I had all the power, considering it was my mother who had come to get me from Cherina's house – I didn't ask to come home. Also, the Social Services were still heavily involved in our lives, so my mother had lost her power to hit me. I was determined to do whatever I wanted and didn't really expect much of a consequence to be honest.

I stumbled home around 3am that morning, drunk and high on cannabis. I rang the doorbell but no-one came to the door. After ringing it again and again, I could hear my mother telling one of my siblings not to open the door. This upset me, so I kept ringing the doorbell over and over until the door was finally opened. I could hear my mother's loud voice cursing me but I didn't care. I went in and headed straight to my bed.

Brixton Beef

Although I was back home, I was still hanging around in the same environment and doing the same things. I got into many fights, including fights with girls in my own area. One of the fights I got into was in Tulse Hill, right near my home. My friend Keisha (RIP) was holding my personal belongings and "lost" all my stuff, including my mobile phone and money. I was then chased down the road by Mackeba and her friends who then attacked me outside my house. I remember calling out for help; when my mother and Aunt

Patsy came to the door, all the girls ran away. They took me inside and cleaned me up.

Most of the fights I got into were territorial fights. People from Brixton didn't like people from Peckham and vice versa. Us being from Brixton and hanging out at Cherina's flat in Peckham was enough to make enemies in both parts of town. In Brixton we were seen as "traitors" and "sell outs". They felt like they had to make examples out of us. In Peckham, they didn't think we belong and so we were disrespecting them by being there. Everyone felt they needed to teach us a lesson for their own status and credibility.

My Life Flashed in Front of Me: The Turning-point

One night in 2002, I was around 17 years old at that time; I was attacked by a group of local girls at the annual Brixton party on Coldharbour Lane. We were known to them and them to us. This was the same group of girls who attacked Cherina at her flat in West Norwood, and since then we were constantly at war. On the last occasion we fought in Brixton next to Natwest Bank. I ended up beating up one of them really badly; she was left with a scar below her left eye, scratches all over her face and broken fake fingernails that also took off some of her real nails. I'd done all of this with my bare hands, and now was their time to get revenge. What made it worse was they'd heard about our time in Peckham, and that upset them even more. I was with my friends Keisha and Ash who don't really like to get into fights that don't directly concern them. My enemies had a huge group of friends that were all hyped up and ready to back them. The arguments were getting quite intense, and I knew they could jump on me at any minute. What made me even more scared, was the fact that they had broken bottles in their hands pointing at me. The more I stood there arguing in my defense the more I could see my life flashing before my eyes. I knew I had family and other friends somewhere in the crowd that would happily defend me, but at that point I couldn't see any familiar faces. I scanned around for a way out but didn't see any.

I thought to myself, is this where it all ends? I felt pretty sure that they were going to have me for breakfast, lunch and dinner – all at the same time. I was so scared and alone in that moment but I felt I had to keep up the front. In my mind, I was prepared to fight to the very end, but all I could see was them slicing me in my face. And they didn't stop there either. I saw myself covered in my blood.

It was all playing out in front of me, yet I was so caught up in the arguments and felt helpless to stopping it from happening. Then suddenly the crowd swayed to the left, then to the right. People were losing their balance and tumbling down over each other. I didn't know what had caused this. But in a split second, I heard a voice telling me to 'Get Out!', and I saw a path made clear for my escape! Without any further thoughts, I ran towards the main road as fast as I could. As I approached KFC, I saw a bus 432 which I knew would go past my house in Tulse Hill. The doors were wide open as if to call me in. I jumped on it and the doors closed behind me. I curled up in one of the corners until the bus stopped outside my house. I got off and ran home; I was still so scared. In this moment, I knew I couldn't carry on like this, something had to change. I needed help but I didn't know where to get it.

Kay – a Guardian Angel?

The next morning laying in my bed, I remembered how Kay had been there for me. He had always wanted to spend more time with me but I always made excuses about how busy I was because I preferred to spend the time with my friends. I also knew he wouldn't approve of the things I was getting up to. But in a moment like this, I knew my friends couldn't give me the help I needed, so I called Kay and told him what had happened. He came and picked me up and took me to spend the day with him. I got involved in his trading business, helping to buy, sell and clean up electronic appliances such as fridges, freezers and washing machines. He gave me a lot of money for my contribution which I could've used to buy anything I wanted, but I chose to buy weed. I didn't have to think about food or clothes as Kay bought these for me, and topped up my phone. I was still living at home with no financial responsibilities; savings wasn't something I'd thought about, so I spent it all on my smoking habits.

During our time together Kay talked to me a lot, asking me questions about my current and future circumstances. I didn't tell him about my extreme past because of the fear of being judged, disliked or rejected as a result. It was obvious to me that he saw better in me than I'd seen in myself. I didn't feel like he was doing it for what he could get in return unlike all the other bupses and men in my life.

It was strange how our relationship developed from where it started. From initially treating him like just another bupse, to being a romantic one where I felt cared for and protected. His ugliness didn't matter to me as much anymore, as I could see pass that to the beautiful person inside. However, I didn't really enjoy having sex with him, maybe because of his age and grey hair. Or maybe it was the way he sucked on my lips so hard that reminded me of Ken, the monster from my past. I thought I owed him. Out of obligation, I wanted so much to please him that I didn't even think about whether I liked it or what made ***me*** happy. What I needed was a friend, not a boyfriend.

I was satisfied knowing that he was getting some pleasure out of our sex life. That's the least I thought I could offer him in return for his invested time and effort in me, especially when no-one else seemed to care. I felt like I needed to maintain his interest, otherwise I'd lose everything he was giving me. The best way I knew how, was via sex. We spent around 12 hours a day, six days a week together. On Sundays he went to church in white robes. I'd usually see him briefly on Sunday evening before he went home. It's interesting that he never invited me to his church, but he did influence me to start going back to my own church as I'd "lost my way".

I'd been going to my local Seventh Day Adventist Church since around the year 2000. Initially I was a devoted Christian and went to church every Saturday in Brixton. I never opened up to anyone there about my real challenges. From a little girl in Jamaica, church was somewhere I felt clean and worthy regardless of what I'd experienced. I saw it as a place of peace and happiness to connect with the Higher Power, God. Sometimes, my attendance was non-existent whereas at other times, I went every week. As Kay maintained his Christian duties whilst being with me, I thought it would be good if I did the same too.

The fact that Kay didn't seem all too keen to have sex more than once or twice a month, made me wonder if it had anything to do with his Christian beliefs; although in my church you're either allowed to have it or not. Only married couples were allowed to have sex. So, I still couldn't place my hand firmly why Kay was like this, but whatever the reason, it just made me wanted to give him my body more. When I questioned him about the frequency of our sex life, he said he didn't want to have sex too often because he wanted to keep enjoying it like it was our first time, and didn't want to lose interest. I didn't really know how to take it, except "Kay knows best." I would be waiting for him anytime he wanted it.

Mentoring 101

Kay would often use normal day to day situations to build context around his guidance and advice to me. For example, one day we were driving down Brixton High Street when we saw a man peeing on the wall outside the KFC in the middle of the day. He asked me what I thought of that man, and I remember saying pure negative things such as "He's a tramp! He has no manners or respect. No one will respect him after doing that." Kay then looked across the street and saw man #2 dressed in full suit carrying a briefcase. He asked what I thought of man #2? My response was much more positive, I said "He looks very important, like he's got a respectable job and people listens to him." Kay then pointed out that my opinions – wrong or right – were based on my perceptions of these two men. He further explained that my perceptions were also based on the image and behavior I observed from each man.

He said:

"For all we know, it could be the other way around – although highly unlikely because a an educated man usually behaves different to an uneducated man. People tend to judge and treat you according to what they see."

I listened to him. I didn't feel like he was judging me or telling me what to do. Instead, he was sharing his knowledge and it was up to me to decide what to do with it. He touched something inside of me which reignited my passion for learning. I knew I was capable of achieving more and I wanted more, for me.

Feeling like he was going to guide me along the way was motivating and made me believe it was possible. Soon after, I found myself breaking away from my friends and coming away from the street life completely. I had new plans to go to College to redo my GCSE's; then A Levels and then to University. I wasn't sure what I wanted to become but I thought it would have something to do with numbers such as an Accountant. I knew my mother would be happier about that kind of career as opposed to becoming a Maths teacher. She said teachers don't earn much money. However, I knew I would figure it out along the way.

By 18 years old, my future looked so bright and exciting. Kay proposed to me and of course I said yes! I still had so much doubt about our future plans, but I took the leap and went ahead, trusting and believing in Kay to guide and support me. To help me focus on my education, Kay promised to give me an additional £50.00 per week for five days of lunch money. He was already financially supporting me, and so, I had no reason to doubt his promises. I felt I had nothing to lose and everything to gain from having him by my side.

He helped me to think bigger and better about myself. Up to that point, I'd lost complete hope of any future ahead of me; I couldn't even see myself in my 40's or older. My reality was that I'd soon either end up dead or in prison. And until that night at Brixton carnival, I didn't seem to care where I ended up. I know now, that wasn't my destiny. I came here for a much higher purpose. I'm so grateful to the Higher Power for fulfilling my needs at that moment in time through Kay. If it hadn't been for the support I received through Kay, I probably wouldn't be here to tell this story. I'm so grateful for the guidance, protection and intervention that helped me overcome these obstacles on my path.

Lambeth College

Sadly, Kay didn't stick around for much longer! He was there for me in my first few months at Clapham Centre, Lambeth College. He kept all his promises up to that point. He would even pick me up from home in the mornings and take me to College sometimes. And he was always there to pick me up after class. He was the only one outside of college that I could consistently talk to about my challenges in class or with my course work. I also shared my thoughts and feelings about the people I was around at college. He genuinely seemed to care. I never felt judged by him, and he always showed interest in what I had to say probing and using each circumstances as opportunities to guide me further.

My friends Cherina, Sarah and Ash would complain that they never got to see me anymore, and say Kay was controlling me. They believed he was making himself be everything to me so I wouldn't want to be around anyone else! But I didn't care because I recognized that Kay had awoken something positive in me. Something I thought had died in me. I never thought I could feel like this again: eager to learn, optimistic and hopeful. I felt alive without taking the kind of negative risks and temporary fix I was used to. Through him, I was finding direction and my life's purpose. I felt great and didn't lack for anything – except on the romantic side of things. I didn't feel he was that interested in sex; he set boundaries about when and how often we would have sex which I felt was weird. Every man I'd known wanted sex, and more of it. It frustrated me how much I wanted him.

I was doing really well at College. Seeing as I'd left school with no GCSE's, I was building my confidence around my plans to re-do my GCSE's, then A-Levels and then University. University seemed very far-fetched at the time but I kept focused on the huge opportunity I felt I was being given to retake my GCSE's and to create a better future for myself.

I chose to do the following 5 subjects: Mathematics, English, Business, Accounting and Information Technology (IT). Unlike my sister Joy, I'd always had a thing for numbers, but I hated English. I only chose it because I was told I had to. When the day came and I finally passed English with a 'C', it was the best feeling ever, because I thought I'd never have to study it again! I never considered I'd actually have to use most of what we were taught in English throughout my life. I knew how to construct a basic sentence verbally and in writing, but I had no interest in being bugged down with all the other ins and outs. Little did I know that communication of any form in English is all about the English language and literature. Seeing as communication is one of the biggest areas of our lives, I guess living in this country, English Studies should be too. Also, I can now see how important it is to tell our stories and I'm seeing how English studies plays a huge part in effective storytelling. It's also relevant in my everyday life such as sending an email, or writing an article or an event publication, etc.

On the other hand, I knew numbers would be more practical and useful in my day-to-day life and future career. But sitting there in my Mathematics exam, my brain wasn't as sharp as it once was at school in Jamaica. I had to now rely on a calculator to work out answers to what should have been simple questions for me.

However, I passed my GCSE's with B's in Mathematics, Business Studies and IT, and C's in English and Accounting. I was very proud of myself for this achievement, that it motivated me to do even better in my A Levels. I was now starting to think of University as a possible option for me.

Kay: MIA

One really big challenge I experienced just before doing my GCSE exams, was that Kay just disappeared! I was absolutely devastated! I called his phone and he didn't pick up or call me back, which was so unlike him. I thought something had happened to him. I was encouraged by my college friends to visit his place. I saw his uncle who told me Kay had travelled back to Nigeria, and they didn't know when he'd be back. My automatic reaction was to give up my new life because I didn't think I could do it without him. HE was my motivator from the start. I believed that HE was the one who planted the seed and created this new life for me. I felt completely lacking within myself without him. My confidence, self-esteem and self-belief took a punch. I didn't know if I was going to get through this or how!

My fairytale life was over, just like that. We didn't even have a fight or anything. At first, I thought I was dreaming, but with each moment that went by without him, I realised more and more that he not coming back. I was so angry and upset with him, myself, God and everything around me. I stayed in my room, smoked weed, drank alcohol, played sad heartbreak songs and cried everyday. I used to hear stories about African men having multiple wives, and so I assumed he'd returned back to his.

Thankfully by then, I had some really good girlfriends at College who reassured me that Kay would've wanted me to continue my studies, even if he wasn't around. They advised that I should do it for myself and no-one else. Thinking about what they said, I reflected on how remarkable the recent changes had been in my life, and although losing my best friend, mentor and fiancé felt like the rug had been pulled from underneath my feet, he had given me so much depth and understanding that I started to believe I could at least try to continue on without him. I felt that all his efforts would have been a complete waste if I'd just given up, and I didn't want to disappoint him. I believed he would come back one day and so, I wanted him to be even more proud of me when returned.

I later understood that this was a crucial part of my life where I had to decide to keep pushing forward for me and no-one else, not even Kay. Kay served his purpose in helping me to build a strong foundation and increased self-worth and self-belief. He helped to boosted my confidence and motivated me to do positive things that I enjoyed doing. For that, I'll be eternally grateful. But now it was time that I did it for me. I needed to put me first. After a while, it felt kind of amazing! I believed more in my future as the path ahead became brighter and brighter.

I didn't have a job and I knew I'd struggle financially. After completing my GCSE exams, I applied for some jobs. Within a couple of weeks, I had two offers: one from Sainsbury's supermarket, and the other as an office-based Market Researcher at Synovate Ltd in Kennington. I chose the latter because I could see myself more in an office than standing on my feet in a supermarket. Also, the Market Research was much more flexible due to it being a zerohour contract, and so I felt more confident that I'd be able to work it around my college life. Securing this job, I introduced many of my friends to this work, even Joy too! Now that I had a flexible and well-paid job, all I had to do was go back to college after the summer break and keep doing what I was doing – but this time, for me.

Grooming

"Grooming is when someone builds a relationship, trust and emotional connection with a child or young person so they can manipulate, exploit and abuse them. Children and young people who are groomed can be sexually abused, exploited or trafficked.

Anybody can be a groomer, no matter their age, gender or race. Grooming can take place over a short or long period of time – from weeks to years. Groomers may also build a relationship with the young person's family or friends to make them seem trustworthy or authoritative." [26]

Returning back to college after the summer break of 2004, I continued to pursue my A-levels. This was a big step for me and I still had a lot of self-doubts. However, my new sense of aspiration, inspiration and motivation was more empowering. I started to feel like I could do anything I wanted – the sky was the limit! I felt in control of my future and knew I wanted more out of life.

I found myself being mentored by my Business Studies teacher; Ivan was a tall, slim, over 50 - Caucasian man with a full head of white hair. He took me under his wings by giving me extra lessons after class. When I needed additional money because work was slow, he offered me some shifts at his office, which was located behind his family home in Wimbledon. He ran his own business, training teachers through conferences and workshops. At first, I worked alone doing admin for him such as printing off letters, putting them in envelopes and posting them. This may sound simpler than it was, considering I had to do thousands of them manually. The pay was really good, and I was even happier when he agreed to allow one of my college friend to help, because I knew she'd appreciate the extra cash too.

---

26 https://www.nspcc.org.uk/what-is-child-abuse/types-of-abuse/grooming/#at-risk

The other teachers noticed how different Ivan was with me and my friends, especially when they heard about him regularly taking us for lunch outside the college building. I believe it made them uncomfortable enough to talk to us directly, warning us that this behaviour wasn't normal. They also asked us specific questions about our dealings with him, but we had not one bad word to say. We admitted we were a bit suspicious at first too, but he'd been nothing but helpful, kind and supportive.

I guess I should've listened to the teachers! Unbeknown to me at the time, I was "being groomed" by Ivan. He later began making advances when he must have felt comfortable enough to get away with it. I suppose he did get away with it in a way, because this is the first time, I'm breaking my silence about it. I mean, at the time, I told my friends some of the things he started saying and doing to me but no one else knew. Ivan often invited me to accompany him at his teacher training conferences – mostly at Friend's House in Euston, London. Sometimes he'd ask me to help out at the events, running chores. Other times he'd invite me to speak or co-host the event. I knew these opportunities were amazing, and they took me so far out of my comfort zone that I'd always request for my main two College friends to join me. I knew one of my friends would always say yes because she was also affected by the reduction in hours at the same workplace plus, the pay from Ivan was really good. We'd get about £100.00-£150.00 per day for doing what sometimes felt like nothing. I started to do my driving lessons at this time and so the extra cash helped to cover this additional expense.

After a while, it became more challenging to keep getting him to agree to my friend coming along. Before I'd even say anything, he'd tell me that he only needed me. At the time, I assumed it was something to do with money, although I couldn't be sure because he seemed to be making a lot of money from his business. I say this because of the admin work I would still do at his office on occasions, so I had more insight into his business operations.

One day he invited me to host one of his conferences at Friend's House. I was so excited and scared at the same time, this was huge! I didn't think I was capable of hosting his conference by myself, but I agreed because he seemed to believe in my capabilities and didn't seem worried at all. On the day, I sat on the stage with him and the other speakers facing hundreds of trainee teachers in the audience, which was pretty scary. We sat on a rectangular shaped table with long table cloths that covered all of the bottom half of our body. Ivan ensured his seat was right next to mine, to my left. I was responsible for telling the audience what to expect throughout the day and for introducing each speaker. When the speakers were giving their presentations, Ivan would use his feet to fumble with mine under the table. This made me so uncomfortable as I didn't know how to take what he was doing. Looking at him, he seemed so calm and in control of himself, you'd never know what he was doing under the table. I kept looking in the audience nervously to see if anyone was watching us. I noticed a mature white woman in the front row with a strange look on her face, staring directly at me. Although I didn't know for sure, I convinced myself that she knew what was going on, and this made me so nervous and panicky. But I felt stuck where I was, and thought there was nothing I could do about it. At one stage his hand was on my thigh, as he whispered in my ear, inviting me for something to eat after the conference. It was normal for him to take me to eat afterwards but on this occasion, I couldn't wait for the event to be over so I could go home. I told him I had something to do after, so couldn't stay. It seems the whispering brought attention to us, as two more ladies were now staring at me with a similar look to the first lady. Ivan must have noticed these women watching, so he stopped whispering and started writing me little 'secret messages' on folded pieces of paper instead. In his messages, he was having casual conversation with me such as "What are you doing after the event? Can't you join me for a quick drink?" He'd also send me compliments such as "You're a natural at hosting", "You're doing a brilliant job", and "The audience loves you!" He also sent messages that made me chuckle, like when he was criticizing one of the guest speakers. I couldn't understand how he had the audacity to behave this way in front of everyone. It certainly made me feel uncomfortable and reminded me of past experiences with my step-dad Ken – he commanded me to be part of his games. I felt powerless to do anything, not that I would've done anything right there and then, because I was too worried about public humiliation and what people would think of me. So, I did my best to manage my emotions as I continued to host the event. At lunchtime I was invited to eat with Ivan and some of his associates, but I made an excuse that I had to make a very important phone call, and that it would take up most of the lunch break. Ivan accepted my excuse, but said I should come and find him afterwards. I agreed, but avoided him until when the event resumed. He said he was looking for me to introduce me to some of his friends who were very impressed with my hosting. I knew he could've opened new doors for me but I overlooked it as if it was nothing. Instead, I told him I would love to meet his friends at the end of the event.

Ivan and I returned to our seats, and new speakers were invited to join us on stage. He continued with his unwanted behaviour of using his feet to play with mine under the table. His hands touched my legs and made my skin crawl. It was the most uncomfortable feeling, and it was all happening in front a room full of professional strangers. Ivan wrote me another note, but I pretended to be distracted so I didn't have to read it straight away. I didn't even want to imagine what was written in the note he so carefully folded in front of me. He used his foot to touch mine to get my attention, and then indicated towards the secret note using his eyes and head.

When I opened the note, it read "Please, just one drink!" I knew he was asking me to have a drink with him after the event, but I just smiled at him as if to say "I wish!" He then came closer into my private space to whisper in my ear about a bar across the road with nice music, which he thought I'd love. I felt so pressured and not taken seriously. It was hard for me to react unkindly to Ivan because he spoke so softly to me, always with a smile on his face. He made me think that it wasn't his fault he enjoyed my company, and at this point, I thought he hadn't really done anything wrong. I even considered the possibility that it was all in my head, and that I was making my own self uncomfortable, perhaps because of my past experiences. Whatever the case, I couldn't stand the thought of being around Ivan after the event, because I realized that somehow, he was starting to make me feel worse inside.

As soon as I finished at the event, I jumped on the train and went home. After a couple of spliffs with some Wray and Nephew Jamaican white rum, I soon forgot about Ivan and his dirty-minded games. The next day, I couldn't actually articulate what Ivan had done wrong. Apart from how I felt inside, I didn't have much to go off, and I wasn't sure if he was completely to be blamed for how I was feeling. I decided to give him the benefit of the doubt, as he had been so good to me and was still my teacher.

At college, he was still nice and friendly to me, like nothing had happened. He continued to support me in many special ways, such as giving me a few hundred pounds towards my housing deposit for University as I needed help raising the balance. He also helped me with some of my first-year assignments. And I knew I could talk to him about any aspect of my University work.

It didn't end there, as Ivan and I kept in contact throughout University. In fact, a few months after finishing Uni, I moved back to Croydon. I was having a house-warming party which I'd told him about in conversations, not expecting he would want to be invited. But he was insistent on coming. He said he had a house-warming gift that he wanted to drop-off on his way to wherever he was going. He said he would quickly pass by and drop off my gift early so I could continue getting ready for my party. I wasn't comfortable with the thought of Ivan coming to my house. It definitely felt like crossing whatever boundaries where still there. However, because of his persuasive nature, I thought it probably wouldn't hurt if I met him outside, collected my gift and go back inside. I gave him my address which must have given him the impression that it was fine to come. He turned up at my house before my other guests had arrived, just as he said he would. To ensure he definitely wouldn't gain entrance to my flat, I told him I was having a lingerie party and only my girlfriends were invited. He suggested he would only come in for a short while then leave. I politely rejected his suggestion and told him I had to go, as my friends had turned up early and were inside waiting for me. He finally left after giving me the gift he'd brought me, but not before rearranging to return a few days later and giving me a big kiss on both sides of my cheeks. In that moment, I felt as if I was in a relationship with him which I hadn't consented to. It made me so uncomfortable how an old, mature and professional guy like Ivan could come across so creepy and unnatural.

The worst part was, I didn't feel I could tell my friends the full story because I thought they'd look at me weird and question me like, why am I inviting or encouraging a teacher to come to my house? Or why haven't I spoken out about my dissatisfaction and discomfort over his behaviour? But the truth was, I'd asked myself these same questions over and over again and "I don't know" was the only answer I came to. I couldn't tell my friends because I wasn't ready to face these questions, I was certain they'd ask. So, I kept it all to myself until this very moment of sharing it in this book.

Looking back now, I can clearly see how Ivan had been seducing me from day one. A huge part of me felt subdued under his will, power, control and influence over me. Ivan entered my life at a time when I'd just lost Kay – an older guy who meant so much to me and did so much for me. Ivan seemed to have indirectly assumed the role of Kay in my life, in that he always had time for me as my teacher, but he also became my friend and employer. Through all these roles, he seemed to go over and above to support and encourage me. He made me feel special and worthy. He even gave me money when I was very desperate, for my accommodation at Uni. Just like Kay, I felt like I owed him, but I never imagined he was doing all of this because he expected sexual favours in return. I hated feeling deceived! I'd rather he'd approached me on a more genuine level and let me decide, just like I decided with Kay. But of course, he knew it was wrong, especially as he was my teacher and I wouldn't have agreed, so he used his power and control over me to lower my guard, and then he struck when he thought he had me where he wanted.

I'm so grateful that by then I was no longer the helpless little girl that guys could do what they want and get away with it. I'm grateful that I understood enough to realize that my boundaries where being crossed, and I'm glad I was finally able to enforce them. By turning Ivan away from my doorstep that night, I took back my power and chose to never see him again. I know he did try to contact me, but I ignored his messages and calls. It's been over 10 years now since I last heard from him.

When I think of Ivan now, a part of me thinks I should've listened to the other teachers at my college who warned me about him. The other part of me embraces all my lessons I've learnt from my experiences, and contributions to different stages of my life – not just from Ivan, but from everyone else that has entered my life.

It has ALL helped to make me who I am today, and I love who I am today!

Immigration Barriers

Before I could go to University, I had to face the next biggest obstacle in my life! That is, as an international student, I'd have to pay thousands of pounds in international fees to be able to attend University! My family didn't have that kind of money and the only way around it was to attend as a 'home student'. That's where the problem was, because my mother had been waiting for years to get a response from the Home Office regarding our application for our Indefinite Leave To Remain in the UK.

If this application was successful, it would give us some entitlement around the benefit system, housing, employment and education - including the fact that I would gain easier access to University being a home student. By this time, I was in my last year of college. Having already applied as a home student to various Universities of my choice, I was aware that they were happy to accept me pending my final A-level results as well as proof of my UK status. We'd been in the UK for approximately six years, with our Home Office application pending for around five years. I felt time was running out for me, so I had to act. Problem is, I didn't know what to do or who to turn to. Furthermore, we have a saying in Jamaica, "don't tell people yuh business or else dey will use it against yuh!" I knew I had to tell someone but I didn't know who to trust because breaking my "family secret" was forbidden. By letting people know we were undocumented, we feared they would alert the authorities and send us back home. For me, this wasn't even an option. Do I risk my family being sent back to Jamaica, loosing everything here and going back into the home of my childhood abuse and violence OR not going to University which meant not accomplishing my goals and possibly falling back onto the streets? I was so torn! Not realising my dreams seemed worse than everything else!

I decided to open up to my Accountancy teacher Angelica. She was a short Jamaican lady who had looked out for me in the past, especially with Ivan. At Parent's Evening my mother and Angelica seemed to get on well too. I thought of her as trustworthy and familiar enough with our Jamaican culture and laws of this Country, to advise me confidentially. Having spoken to her, she advised me to speak with my Law teacher, which I did. He advised me to speak to my local MP, and also guided me how to contact my MP as I had no idea how to do things like that. Now that I had some direction of where to get help, the big decision was whether to open up to government officials believing they could send me back home.

Although I had no real evidence to guarantee the best outcome, I still decided to move forward. To me, this was a "do or die" situation. I was too close to realising my potential, to let anything stop me. At this stage I wanted to become a lawyer and I knew I had to go to University to get my degree. I remember relying on my religious beliefs that God had something in store planned for me and He wouldn't have brought me this far just to leave me. That song 'Can't Give Up Now', by Mary Mary played over and over in my mind. "I've come too far to turn back now." I cried. I prayed and cried some more. I just couldn't give up. What would my life look like? I couldn't bear to think about it. I had to try!

I searched for my local MP's details over the internet. I came across Lambeth Council's website, where I found out that Keith Hill was the MP for Streatham which covered Clapham Park, where I lived. I wrote down his details and called his office to make an appointment. I was so nervous but I explained to the lady who answered the phone that I would like to see Mr Hill as I needed help with my home office application urgently before I could go to University. She gave me an appointment for a week later. I went to see him on my own. I sat in his office anxiously waiting to be called. When I heard my name I jumped up, and walked into the room where he sat waiting. I closed the door behind me and sat down. He was a white Caucasian man of authority with glasses. I was really scared and anxious over what's about to happen. In fact, I was dying inside. I felt the knots in my tummy. I was hot and flustered, with sweety palms.

The negative voices in my head were going wild telling me: "Don't say anything", or "Now they'll all know!", "What will my mother say?" "It will all be your fault!" and warning me that "You're gonna regret this!"

I composed myself and with a smile on my face to cover my anxiety, I opened my mouth and started talking. Once I started, I couldn't stop. He took notes and asked me further questions to get a clearer picture of my UK status. At the end of the meeting he told me to book another appointment with his receptionist when I should come back with further information and specific documents. He gave me a list of the things he needed. Overall, he seemed very positive that my family and I had the right to obtain legal settlement based on a recent changes in law that had passed in year 2000. He wanted to see our documents to confirm this before saying anything else. If he was right, he would happily contact the Home Office on our behalf.

This was VERY positive news! It was enough to settled my nerves and much more than I could even dream of. However, to move forward, I'll now have to get my mother's help. I would have to admit to her that I'd broken our silence and opened up to government officials about our circumstances. I'd also need her to give me copies of our documents to give it to the MP. I had no idea how I was going to achieve this alive but I booked another appointment to return in two weeks'. During that time, I waited for the right moment at home and planned my words very carefully. Finally, I built up the courage and "let the cat out the bag!" I told my mother the full story and how the MP said he could help but first, he needed our documents. I handed her the list from the MP. I sat in anticipation of her reaction, ready to escape through the door. But to my surprise, she responded very well. In fact, she happily gave me the documents I needed and answered the MP's questions. I was so surprised! I was dancing on top of the world. I couldn't believe how easy that was, considering everything I'd built up inside me. And from that point, everything else went smoothly.

I attended my second appointment, again by myself, but this time, more confidently. I gave the MP all the information and documentation he required. A couple of weeks later, we received a copy of the letter he had written to the Home Office which was shortly followed by a response from the Home Office. I couldn't believe how quickly they responded considering how long my mother had been waiting to hear from them through her solicitor. The letter from the Home Office confirmed our eligibility for our Indefinite Leave to Remain but first, they needed us to complete a questionnaire. I don't remember the questions asked, just that all of our names were on it!

About a month after sending back the completed questionnaire, my mother received a phone call from her lawyers telling her they'd received a letter from the Home Office giving our family legal Rights to Remain Indefinitely in the UK. This was by far, the happiest day of my life! It renewed my faith and trust that somethings do work out. Miracles do happen. I can achieve what I set my mind to. I did it, not just for myself, but also my family too. I concurred by fears, push forward and got the results I wanted. For someone like me with my background - this was probably the biggest boost to my self esteem and confidence knowing I did it by myself with help from the Higher Power. The last biggest thing in my life was leaving an abusive environment to come to the UK, but this topped it on so many levels.

Words can't really express the gratitude, relief, joy and happiness this brought to my family and I. Plus it came just in time for me to go to University as a Home student. But before I went off to the University of Brighton, my family and I visited Jamaica for the first time since immigrating here.

Family Holiday to Jamaica

I had mixed emotions about returning to Jamaica. I was so happy to go on our first family holiday and return home to Cottage Bottom. Everything looked and felt different, like it was the same but not the same. My attachment to things had somehow changed. I saw things more clearly now. It's so weird to explain. And when I saw Mark, I wasn't attracted to him anymore. I didn't even want to spend the night at Cottage. Instead, I wanted to stay in a hotel! However, stayed at Miss Bee's house in Mount Airy (close to where we used to live too before moving to Heskit).

Miss Bee is a lovely woman; she always had been and still is to this day. I remember she was one of the few people that spoke out against Ken's violence at the time and did what she could to help my mother and her children. On this occasion, she gave us her home where we stayed for about three weeks. She cooked for us regularly and gave us many things from her shop without requiring us to pay for everything.

Returning back home, many people no longer saw us as "one of them". Instead, we were "foreigners" and had to pay foreigners' prices most places we went. To avoid paying this, we were told by locals not to open our mouth and say a word! "Keep yuh mouth shut!" they said. Even some of the locals treated us differently by wanting everything we wore. If they asked us and we didn't give it to them, they'd be upset and speak badly about us. Some may even steal it from us. This was mainly because they still subscribed to the picture of England sold to us on the TVs in Jamaica, similarly to the mentality I had when I first came to the UK, expecting a big pool at the back of my house. However Miss Bee didn't treat us like that. She had travelled across the world and knew what things were really like including the barriers to settling in and creating a new life in another country, without much help. Also, we were family as far as she was concerned. I didn't feel like she was better or worse than us. Just pure family and she looked after us as such.

It was very uncomfortable for me staying in that area because of all the negative memories it brought back. From my mother being violently abused over and over again, a stone throw away from Miss Bee's house; to that day at the crossroads with my mother and I attempted escape; to the sexual and physical abuse and rape I experienced as a child, along with public humiliation when they found out about the rape; Miss Bev's ill treatment and wrongful accusations of me; to just being fearful of seeing Ken again! There were so many triggers, flashbacks and anxiety weighing me down. The best way I knew to cope through this level of distressing emotions was to smoke weed and drink rum right around the clock, party hard and have sex!

Déjà Vu

The day came when Ken finally showed his face. I was in Miss Bee's bar when he walked in. As I saw him, I quickly left. I suppose my automatic reaction here was flight! I almost couldn't breathe. I didn't want to cause any commotion as I couldn't stand public humiliation or wondering what they would be thinking. I went into my room and stayed there for a while. I thought to myself that he looked the same, except a little older with some more grey hair. I tried to fight the flashbacks and just be ok with the situation.

After a while, as I was leaving the house to smoke a spliff when I bucked up with Ken, in one of the rooms! I thought I was dreaming! I froze! I almost died inside! It was almost like it was happening all over again, except it wasn't. He hadn't even touched me. It was a completely different situation yet the shock of seeing him so unexpectedly in the house made me feel like I was that helpless and hopeless broken little girl again. He must have noticed my reaction, when he broke the silence and casually told me that my mother had sent him for something. Without responding, I quickly escaped through the front door and went for a walk, smoking away my troubles. I can't remember where I went, I just knew I smoked a lot! By the time I returned, he was gone.

He came back to the house a few more times whilst we were there. But I never encountered anything like the shock on the first day. My mother was surprisingly calm and forgiving of him. I'm not aware of her doing or saying anything to make it any easier for me (or any of my siblings). But over the time, I learnt to brush it under the carpet too, and just tried to be ok with it, or at least that's what I told myself. My sister Joy and I had a joint birthday party in Jamaica Summer 2006 and Ken even came and made my favorite soup: Manish water. My body would often freeze or I would feel scared around him. But I ignored these signals and instead spent time with people who made me laugh such as Joy, Woodie, Adam and Fargo.

I knew there was not much more I could do about the situation and I didn't want any more drama on our holiday, especially as I knew we'd be leaving him behind again, and I'd be starting a bright future at University soon.

CHAPTER THREE

Breaking The Silence

Uni Life

Initially I struggled financially to get myself settled because I didn't have the necessary financial support I needed to move away from London and start a new life as a student at the University of Brighton. I needed around £3000 - £5000 to pay for the accomodation costs, as well as books and other things. My family generally struggled to make ends meet, moreover we had just returned from Jamaica in August 2006; in celebration of our permanent UK status. I came back to London with £5 in my pocket which was less than what I needed to buy a box of cigarettes. I remember contacting one of my ex's trying to get some pocket money to go to and from work. To help me prepare for University in September 2006, I had to work really hard doing extra-long hours at Synovate Market Research, at every possible opportunity. I also received a few hundred pounds from my teacher Ivan. Together, I had enough to secure a shared private accommodation next to the main building where I'd be attending my classes. I bought a few resources for my classes such as textbooks, note pads, pens, different colour sticky note, etc. And for my new home, I bought bed covers, pots, plates, cups, utensils, computer, computer table, food shopping etc.

I didn't yet have access to any student loan or grant, but did hoped at least one of them would come through in time for when my first month's rent and bills would become due. I tried to secure a student overdraft but was unsuccessful at the time because of issues to do with my Jamaican passport which many high street banks rejected. So, even with evidence of my UK status, there was still some barriers with my actual paperwork.

On my first day in Brighton, I handed out my CV in many places such as clothes and shoes shops, travel agencies etc. I also signed up to online recruitment agencies such as reed.co.uk and applied for jobs there too. I was offered a retail job on that same day, but I couldn't take it because it conflicted with the timing of my classes.

I remember my first day at Uni, I had mixed emotions. On one hand, I couldn't believe I actually made it. On the other hand, all my classmates were talking about "Fresher's Fair" where they had partied the night before, and where planning to party again that night. I remember walking away from their conversations because I was too busy thinking about how I was going to pay my bills by the end of the month, which was only a couple weeks away.

I was so relieved when I got my first sales job, although I soon hated it because I thought I was more of the customer service type. I liked serving people, not selling to them, especially things I don't believe will benefit them! However, I did what I had to do until I got a better one.

The Calm Before the Storm

By early 2007, things started looking bright for me. Not only did my student loan and grant came through, I'd opened up a new bank account with Lloyds in Brighton and I got immediate access to £2000 student overdraft. Shortly after that, I also secured a job with Lloyds Bank working part time from their office as a Customer Consultant. I remember my first day at the bank; I thought I'd made it in life being a student at Uni and working in a bank. I ended up on one of the best teams with Danny as my manager; Naomi and Lou were my initial friends there who also attended Brighton Uni. Soon after, one of my Uni friends Teni, got a job working there too. My team went out for many drinks after work! The extravagant Christmas parties were the best every year. Within that group, I saw much more drug usage than I'd witnessed in my teenage years on the streets.

I travelled to America on my own for the first time, to see one of my Aunt that lived in Atlanta and a cousin in New York. This entire trip was so fun and adventurous, even when I got stranded in Detroit.

Returning to Brighton, I continued doing my driving lessons, but with slightly different roads (i.e more roundabouts and hills) than in London; it took me much longer to pass my test. I bought my first car, a Volkswagen from Lidia, a Uni friend, so I could practice my driving more often. After one failed theory test, two failed manual tests, many panic attacks and a lot of tears, I officially passed my driving test. I soon bought my first sports car, a Ford Puma and Citroen convertible which reinforced my possibilities. Remembering where I was coming from and where I was at that time, made me so proud of myself and my achievements. I felt happy and successful. I had some good girlfriends around me as well, including Teni, Vivian, Leah, Naomi and Sandra. I was also seeing someone I really liked; generally he was supportive of me, though sometimes it felt like it wasn't worth the stress.

Being in this improved position, I chose to help my family financially and emotionally. I made myself available to help my mother worked through challenges with my siblings. I utilised the skills I'd learnt through work by listening to both sides and coming to reasonable solutions that everyone could agree on. I became the person everyone came to vent, and release built-up tensions, then I would guide them to the solutions. It was so much just like being at work, except that they're my family who I care deeper for. I bought my siblings a lot of gifts on birthdays and Christmas. On normal days, I gave them pocket money. I was happy with my contribution to my family. In my culture, it's the older child's responsibility to look after the younger ones. I was proud of myself that I'd managed to settled into Uni without my family's support, and now, I was in a position to keep up with my responsibilities to my family without the strain.

Earlier Signs

I soon started to notice triggers from my past, such as when my sister Joy received a phone call from her cousin in Jamaica, begging her to tell her dad to leave her alone. I couldn't believe that Ken was still up to his old habits, and it suddenly dawned on me that I may not be his only victim. It felt like I should do something about it, but I felt helpless to revisiting the past. Just the thought of it alone was so overwhelming, I chose to continue blocking it out, hoping it would go away. After all, that's what I'd done all these years. I was having extreme nightmares too. My dreams were so vivid and real! A monster was always chasing me. Each night the monster would take a different form, and the environment would vary but still extreme. For example, one night it was chasing me through fire; another night, I was running over broken bottles or barbwire. I would always run wherever was necessary to escape and it was always chasing me wherever I went. It was usually close enough behind, to have me panicking in deep fear, although it never caught me. My deepest fear at the time was hoping that monster never caught me. I had sleeping difficulties and used alcohol and cannabis to put myself to sleep, but I'd often wake up anxiously in a cold sweat.

I became overly sensitive to the guy I was seeing at the time, starting unnecessary arguments with him. Essentially, I pushed him away enough that the relationship broke down. Believing he was seeing someone else, I started seeing my ex again too, and ended up having on/off relationships with both of them, depending on which one my spirit took to on specific days. I knew things weren't the best, but I was trying to push ahead without anyone suspecting what was really going on. I drank and smoked more. I was too scared to tell anyone and have them look down on me after I'd worked so hard to obtain whatever status I thought I had at the time.

The Ultimate Trigger – My Roof Crashed!

One day in my second year at Uni, I was in my Criminal Law class when the lecturer came in and wrote on the board,

"Today's lesson is about Rape!"

Freeze

It was so unexpected. My roof crashed to the floor! I froze instantly. [27] I was in deep shock with many voices overpowering my mind and going wild in my head - screaming and shouting at me. Some of these voices were shouting that everyone knew what had happened to me. My body was responding to an extremely fearful and publicly humiliating situation that didn't exists outside of my mind. I didn't hear another word from the lecturer for the rest of the class. Although my physical body froze, my mind was racing wild with extreme negative thoughts, flashbacks, screams and a picture of a monstrous version of Ken's face, close up to mine. It was unlike anything I'd ever experience before.

Triggers

I was being triggered! Triggers can come at anytime, and in any shapes or forms through any of our five senses. [28] When it happens, it can disrupt your entire foundation! Everything you experience as a result of the trigger feels so real and can consume your entire mind and body, whilst disconnecting you from your spirit – leaving you feeling completely broken inside. If this ever happens to you, talk to someone. Don't keep it to yourself.

27 https://trauma-recovery.ca/impact-effects-of-trauma/fight-flight-freeze-responses/
28 https://psychcentral.com/lib/what-is-a-trigger/

Self Blame

At the time, I blamed myself for not preparing for this lesson like I'd normally do. I usually know what my next lesson is about. Instead, I was taken completely off guard and now I was involuntarily stuck in mind, having an out of body experience. I sat through the entire class without saying a word or asking a question, which was so unlike me. I don't know how well I masked what was going on internally. I was completely in another world, mentally, whilst still being somewhat aware of my external environment. I was aware that I was still seated in the class. I wanted to run and escape but I couldn't; part of me suggested that it was safer to stay seated. I remember thinking "don't move, otherwise everyone will know you've been raped!" It may sound silly now, but at the time, this was very real for me. I couldn't bear the public embarrassment or the possibility of these thoughts being right. So, I surrendered to my mental battle. I paid the price of "containing my secret" by staying seated. This broke me down even more.

Fight and Flight

I finally came to, when the lecturer said, "This class has been dismissed." I quickly jumped up from my seat without saying a word and escaped down the corridor.[29] My head was pounding, heart was racing and I was breathing so fast. I couldn't hold back the tears. The more I cried, the faster I ran, the hotter I felt and the more of out breathe I was. I didn't notice anyone calling after me, nor did I look back to see if anyone was coming to check on me. I was filled

29 https://trauma-recovery.ca/impact-effects-of-trauma/fight-flight-freeze-responses/ For more information about the fight, flight or freeze response, check out this link.

with too much fear, shame, blame and guilt to care. In that moment, I ended up on my University Counsellor's chair for the first time.

Counselling

For me, this is proof that I was ready to deal with this situation. It doesn't mean I wasn't in pain. In fact, I was going through the most agony. My mind was like a warzone! However if I wasn't ready to face it, I could've went home to my usual drugs and alcohol coping mechanisms. Nobody would've known and nobody would've tried to stop me which means I made that decision for me. We must take the time to recognise and appreciate the positive actions we take even when we didn't think we were strong enough to. We all have it within us. If you don't feel you're there yet. Don't worry. Everyone is at their own pace on their own journey.

Facing my early childhood years of physical abuse, sexual abuse and rape were the biggest challenges of my life! And starting these counselling sessions at that time, was the best thing I could've ever done for myself. For the first few counselling sessions, I was scared, vulnerable and in so much pain. I just cried. She said that was ok. She was calm, patient and nurturing to me. I didn't feel pressured to talk or judged for the way I was being.

Eventually, I started to open up and speak about my pain. After a few more sessions, my counsellor explained that she wanted to refer me for specialist assessment and therapy because she thought my issues were very complex and needed more support than she was able to provide. At first, I was scared to go anywhere else or speak to anyone else about my issues. I felt safe enough inside that room, with that counsellor, at that Uni. Anything else outside of that narrowed perspective would've pose a problem for me, and I definitely didn't want to start all over again. I didn't want to complete any more forms. I didn't trust anyone else, but she convinced me that it was the best thing for me.

PTSD

"The effects of child sexual abuse can be long-lasting and affect the victim's mental health. Victims are more likely than non-victims to experience the following mental health challenges:

- ***About 4 times more likely to develop symptoms of drug (and alcohol) abuse***
- ***About 4 times more likely to experience PTSD as adults***
- ***About 3 times more likely to experience a major depressive episode as adults"*** [30]

Going for the assessment, I remember being in a small room where someone was talking to me and asking me questions. For the most part, I zoned out and was stuck in my own mental warfare. Occasionally, I came to, and answered briefly to some of their questions. I remembered hearing the words Post Traumatic Stress Disorder (PTSD)[31] for the first time, with them making comparison to soldiers who had fought on the battlefield. This was suppose to give me some context as to what I was going through. My mind did feel like a battlefield. I guess I was at war. Who was I fighting? Where was my armor to defend myself in the midst of this mental war?

I was referred for EMDR (Eye Movement Desensitisation and Reprocessing) which is "a fairly new, nontraditional type of psychotherapy. It's growing in popularity, particularly for treating

30 https://www.rainn.org/statistics/children-and-teens
31 https://www.nhs.uk/conditions/post-traumatic-stress-disorder-ptsd/

PTSD. PTSD often occurs after experiences such as military combat, physical assault, rape, or car accidents. [32]

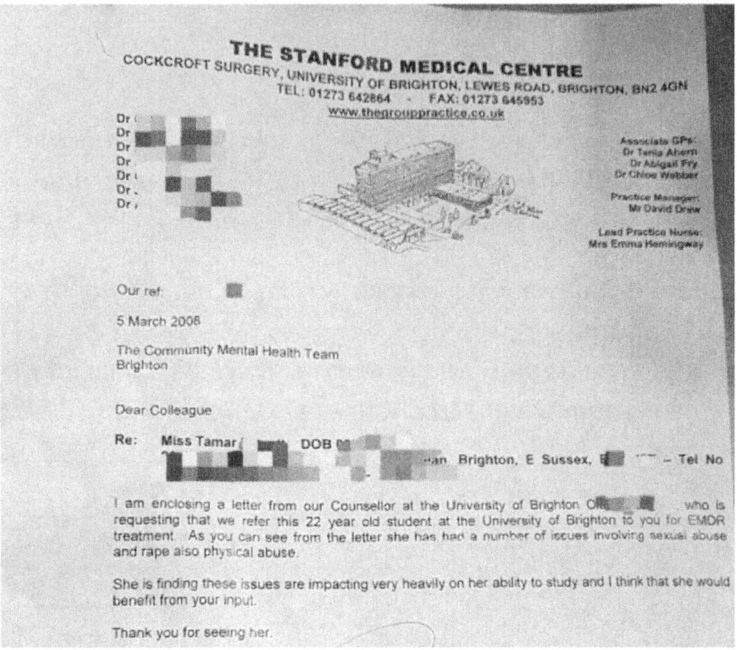
THE STANFORD MEDICAL CENTRE
COCKCROFT SURGERY, UNIVERSITY OF BRIGHTON, LEWES ROAD, BRIGHTON, BN2 4GN
TEL: 01273 642864 - FAX: 01273 645953
www.thegrouppractice.co.uk

Dr [redacted]
Dr [redacted]
Dr [redacted]
Dr [redacted]
Dr [redacted]
Dr [redacted]
Dr [redacted]

Associate GPs:
Dr Tania Ahern
Dr Abigail Fry
Dr Chloe Webber

Practice Manager:
Mr David Drew

Lead Practice Nurse:
Mrs Emma Hemingway

Our ref: [redacted]

5 March 2008

The Community Mental Health Team
Brighton

Dear Colleague

Re: Miss Tamar [redacted] DOB [redacted] Brighton, E Sussex, [redacted] – Tel No

I am enclosing a letter from our Counsellor at the University of Brighton [redacted] who is requesting that we refer this 22 year old student at the University of Brighton to you for EMDR treatment. As you can see from the letter she has had a number of issues involving sexual abuse and rape also physical abuse.

She is finding these issues are impacting very heavily on her ability to study and I think that she would benefit from your input.

Thank you for seeing her.

Additional Mental Health Challenges

I felt extremely overwhelmed like I couldn't cope, so I stopped attending the treatment sessions. My mental health was creating additional barriers for me to receive the help I needed. I also had a constant pain in my chest felt like someone was pulling my heart out of my rib cage. The impact of the trauma [33] was so extreme that I was having regular panic attacks, night terrors and I feared the foundation I'd worked so hard to build was falling apart. I felt unable to allow myself to freely take off my mask and show

32 https://www.webmd.com/mental-health/emdr-what-is-it

33 https://www.nhs.uk/oneyou/for-your-mind/possible-causes#possible-causes-traumatic-events

my vulnerability to the world. It scared me that I'd be judged and rejected, just like the Heskit community had done when they found out I was raped!

Throughout this challenging period, I smoked, drank and binge eat a lot more. I went from smoking a couple of spliffs per day, to smoking right around the clock. And I needed the alcohol to intensifying the buzz in order to block out my thoughts and emotions. When I wasn't smoking or drinking, I was feasting on sweets, cakes, crisps, chocolates, puddings, and ice cream. These foods made me feel so good inside even if it was just temporary. I'd stock up on them and eat whenever and however much I felt like. When I got really full, I'd be too uncomfortable so I'd go and vomit in the bathroom to release myself and start all over again!

I didn't want to leave my house. Not even to go to work or Uni. I ate lots of take away delivery food. Everything got delivered, even my cannabis! Plus, I was having sex with the 'cannabis guy' who also was a student at the University! So, if I didn't have to leave the house, I wouldn't. I could stay in for weeks at a time which just make me feel even more anxious to go out through the door.

Support is available

I remember one of my ex's visited me during one of my many panic attacks at the time. The embarrassment I felt on top of everything else was overwhelming. I still liked him a lot and didn't want him to see me in that state, out of fear of being judged. I didn't want to feel alone, but I wanted to be alone. I could barely manage what what was going on internally moreover be worrying about what me must be thinking of me. I didn't know how to express this when I barely understood how I was feeling. Looking back now, I'm glad he came when he did. I'm also glad I didn't send him back or seemed to have pushed him away too much. He handled it very well. He took me out for a drive in his car. We had to make an immediate stop on the road because I felt like I couldn't breathe and had to get out of the car. As soon as the car stopped, I opened the door and jumped out. I started to walk really fast on the pavement. I thought he was in the car waiting for me until I heard footsteps approaching from behind followed by his calm voice behind me telling me everything will be ok. He told me how strong I was and that I'd get through it. My conscious mind paid him no attention, in fact, I remember thinking "He doesn't know anything so don't listen to him."

I can't remember ever telling him anything about what I was going through, but he said the perfect words for me in that moment. My conscious mind resisted his words and reject his support. I just couldn't let him in, out of fear of more hurt and pain. However my subconscious mind recorded it, and still reminds me of his words every now and again. I'm now very grateful for the support that was expressed through him, although my gratitude was probably non existent at the time..

I carried on walking fast for at least another 10 minutes and he walked behind me until I finally slowed down, and then he walked beside me. I remember us having casual light conversations about everything else other than what was really bothering me, such as the weather and what I wanted to eat. We walked back to his car, grabbed something to eat and then he drove me home.

This is one of my key examples which highlights how our High Power help us face our challenges. IT always know the right people to send our way, the right words to say and the right things for them to do. "They" could be anyone, but more likely to be somebody we have less resistance against and likely to receive the message from them. "They" could be a stranger, a close friend, your pets or even a sign in nature, depending on where you are internally in that moment in time. The emphasis shouldn't be on the person or thing but rather focusing on receiving the support available to us. At the back of this book, I've listed some UK organisations that provides different types of specialist support. You may also seach online for other support in your local area.

Mental Health at Work

"Mental health problems at work are common. At least one in six workers is experiencing common mental health problems, including anxiety and depression." [34]

At this time, everything in my life was changing. I hadn't been off work on long term sickness for nearly a year, and now they were threatening to sack me. My employer requested a medical report from my GP which explained some of the things I was going through. Although my manager at the time seemed emphatic to my circumstances, he was still very clear about the "business needs" and told me he couldn't hold out for much longer without having to sack me for my disability. If I didn't want to be sacked, I'd have to show them some likelihood of me returning to work in the near future. Eventually, I went back to work out of fear of loosing my job. I was worried about my finances as well as completely giving up my lifestyle and status that came with working at the bank.

I pushed myself through much hard times at work. It was even more challenging being there than I would've thought. The country was going through one of its biggest recession in 2008 and banks

34 https://www.mind.org.uk/workplace/mental-health-at-work/taking-care-of-yourself/. If you are experiencing mental health problems at work, check out this link for simple steps you can take to look after yourself and make your workplace mentally healthier.

were under a lot of pressure to make some significant changes for their continued existence. These constant changes affected my mental health even more. It became more evident to me that I shouldn't be at work. I could hardly look anyone in the eyes without feeling like my wound was so open and vulnerable to them. I was mentally slow at processing and storing new training. I regularly felt confused and fearful at work for no apparent reasons. I'd break down in tears at the slightest challenge from customers over the phone. When my manager asked me questions like "What can the workplace do to support you better"; I'd wrap myself in a shell and really just wanted to go back to my desk or home where I could distract myself from how I was feeling – even if it was only short temp.

I felt like I was getting in the way, rather than contributing to the changes at work. All of this delayed my healing process, created more resistance and used up even more of my strength. Eventually it became too much, and so, I had to let go of this work. By that point, I crashed and burned. I found myself having a mental breakdown, buried in a deep dark hole called depression.

My Siblings

My relationship with my mother and siblings had broken down drastically. My step-dad and perpetrator is the father to 4 out of 7 of my siblings. This created an even more complex and emotional situation that we were all victims of. Although each of these four siblings have their individual challenges with their father, my situation was by far the more extreme case, which would naturally cause them to develop even more negative feelings towards both me and their dad. I tried my best to understand things from my siblings' perspective, but I refused to sacrifice my healing and recovery anymore. This is one of the hardest decisions I've ever had to make.

Although I love and care deeply for all my brothers and sisters, I had to put me first. If I don't, who will. By putting myself first, I'm been responsible and accountable for my own happiness for the very first time.

In fact, before my silence was broken, I'd become the core within my family, helping to resolve issues between my mother and siblings or between my siblings themselves. I'd developed individual relationships with each of them, and so, whenever there was a problem, it was easier for me to approach specific members of my family to get their point of view in coming to a holistic solution, or them approaching me to seek my help.

When my silence was broken, there was no one to "keep the family together" seen as I'd assumed that role as the eldest daughter. To make matters worse, my broken silence affected each of them in their own individual way, and everyone was left on their own to deal with their emotions/or not deal with them – in their own way. I can't imagine what that must have been like for them. I am truly sorry that my siblings have had to go through this pain and confusion. Considering how young they still were, I'm sorry I couldn't be there for them, at a time when they probably needed me the most. I've had to accept that I am their sister, not their mother which means it's not my sole responsibility to make them feel better. Although it may feel to them like I'd deserted them, the truth is, I was in such turmoil with my own pain that I was helpless to helping them or anyone else even if I wanted to. I know this has caused some long-term damage between myself and some of my siblings, but over time, I'm confident that this shall pass.

My Mother

In these deepest and darkest moments, all I wanted was my mother to hug and comfort me and tell me everything would be ok. But this felt like the hardest thing for her to do at the time. I knew she'd an extremely tough past her self but I couldn't understand why comforting me in my pain was so difficult for her. As I couldn't understand this, it made me even more angry as the pain from the rejection intensified in my chest. What I found even more painful was feeling like she was blaming me and denying some of what I'd been through as a child. This really confused me to the maximum! It felt like she was standing by and watching my abuse took place all over again without trying to do anything to help. I felt so rejected and neglected by her, the one person I actually wanted help from.

I remember trying so hard to see things from her perspective. Being a natural problem solver, I tried to mediate the situation between my mother and I. As I used to be a member of Brixton Seventh Day Adventist Church – so, I reached out to the pastor and arranged a meeting for my mother and I to discuss our issues and try to resolve them. She's a private person and I wasn't sure how she'd take it when she found out that I got the pastor involved, especially regarding the topic of sexual abuse which is heavily stigmatized in our community. I felt I still had to try to do something to work through it, especially when I heard how my siblings were also being impacted by what was going on. You can imagine my shock when my mother turned up for the meeting! I felt good yet anxious inside that I'd finally set up a platform for her to hear what I had to say, and for the pastor to help me communicate this to her in a way that she may better understand. The meeting wasn't as successful as I'd hoped; my mother and I ended up being at each other's throats, which made it very difficult for the pastor to offer any support.

Suicidal

I left the meeting feeling very angry and distressed. I jumped in my car and drove back to Brighton as fast as I could. I remember the weather was a bit foggy and raining but I didn t care. I wanted so much to get away from her get back into my comfort zone – my room in Brighton. The warzone in my mind was ongoing, and I wished I could end it by cutting off my neck and replacing my head with someone else's. I don't think I wanted to end my life, just the warzone that was going on in my mind. There were so many thoughts, screams and flashbacks with everything going really fast. I couldn't stop or control them.

I was driving over 100 miles per hour on the motorway. A strong thought came in my mind to slow down, but this was instantly followed by another thought saying:

"What's the worst that can happen?"

I heard the voice answering it's own question, in a matter of a fact kind of way, saying,

"I may have an accident and die, or I may get pulled over by the police."

The voice tried to comfort me by saying,

"At least if you die, the mental warzone will end and you won't have to be going through this anymore. If you get arrested by the police, you'll sleep in a cell and the punishment will distract you from how you're feeling now."

Whichever one had happened, I seemed to accept it would be better than how I was feeling. So I stepped on the gas and drove even faster! I don't know how I arrived back home in Brighton safely that day! I remember crying uncontrollably as I burst through the front front door of my house. My friend Vivian saw me and came to comfort me. Within a few hours or drinking and smoking I had calmed down, but the pain in my heart didn't budge.

A few days later I realized where I was going wrong which was making things worse for me. I was trying to help her to help me. I had to accept I can't help someone who didn't want to be helped, as challenging as that may be. I eventually had to accept the fact that the only person I could help was myself. Since then I chose to focus on my own self-healing whilst appreciating how challenging this journey is for some others to even begin.

You see, being a "fixer" has many benefits, however this must be balanced out with the ability to focus on one's own self. By growing through these challenges, I was able embrace and appreciate this lesson. We can't fit anyone. We can only support those who are ready to receive, having already supported ourselves. Each of us have to come to our own understanding that there is a problem and willing to work on ourselves to grow through it. By facing up to our own challenges we're inspiring others to do the dame. I believe that's the best we can do.

University

I'd fallen behind in my class and I was too embarrassed to tell my lecturers what I was going through.

My studies still meant a great deal to me, so I did my best and worked extra hard to catch up. Although I did amazingly well and finished Uni with a 2:1 LLB Law and Business degree, I still beat up on myself and even saw myself as a failure. Before that triggering incident in class that day, I was predicted a 1st class degree and I knew I could've achieved it, but for what I was going through. This may not make sense to some people, so let me elaborate:

On one hand, I knew I was wrong to compare myself to other students who graduated with a 2:1 – many of them didn't seem to work as hard as I felt like I had to. I also felt it was so unfair that I had to push through so much to complete my degree and yet still there was no extra reward. I didn't get what I thought I deserved - a 1st class degree!

On the other hand, I blamed myself for allowing my past to dictate my future in this way. But yet again, I felt helpless to how it impacted which made me so angry and resentful.

I can now see that I was undermining my efforts and feeling insufficient because that's how I was used to feeling. For example when my mother compared my behaviour to other children or say things like, "Why you always get a 'B'? Why can't you get an 'A' like your sister or the other brighter children?" Looking back now, I now realise know how silly these self-critiquing thoughts were.

At the end of the day, I was under immense stress and pressure. I could've easily given up or deferred my studies, but I didn't. I recovered and completed my degree as expected, which took a massive amount of strength, courage and tenacity. Instead of beating up on myself, I should celebrate these qualities and the evidence that shows they exist within me.

Staying in my own lane and not comparing my journey to anyone else, I feel very fulfilled knowing I have the capacity to accomplish my desires, regardless of the challenges. Furthermore, its because of these challenges why I've now developed a range of effective tools and processes to better manage my challenges. I've proven to myself that I can fight my battles without the right armor. So now, imagine what I can achieve with having an effective process in place to deal with challenges; life can only get better!

Graduation Day

Setting aside the mixed emotions I had at the time about my actual grade, I was excited about my graduation day. I felt proud of myself for how far I'd come, and to be part of such an important and special day. My friends and I talked about which of our family members we were going to invite to our graduation. Tickets were limited to two or three friends/family per graduate and had to be bought in advance. I knew I wanted my sister Joy as I knew she was happy for me. I also liked the idea of my mother coming, but I wasn't sure how that would play out considering our ups and downs at the time. Anyways. I invited her and she said yes. On the day of my graduation, I drove over 50 miles from Brighton to Balham in London to pick up my mother and sister and then drove back to Brighton where the graduation ceremony was been held. I remember being very upset on my way back to Brighton because of arguments and negativity between my mother and I. I felt so overwhelmed and feeling unappreciated and unloved.

Although I was focused on getting this from my mother, I now realised, I wasn't appreciating or loving myself, and so no one else can give us what we don't already give to ourselves.

By the time I got back to Brighton I was not on speaking terms with my mother and I just wanted the day to be over. I picked up my gown and sat with my class waiting for my name to be called so I can collect my certificate and drop my family back to London. That's exactly what I did without even stopping to take one picture. I was just so angry. I blamed my mother for ruining my graduation day and I blamed myself for allowing her to do that to me. I remember seeing some of my friends at the graduation and they could tell I'd been crying, but I didn't even want to talk to them. I was done with the day. I dropped my mother and sister back to the house in Balham. After that I went to see my cousin Cherina and my friend Sarah, told them about what had happened whilst drinking and smoking my pain away.

I spent the next couple of days planning my joint graduation and birthday party. It was meant to be a glamourous evening with food, entertainment and dancing. All expenses were fully paid for by myself. Friends and family members who were invited where told to dress up and come to celebrate my graduation and birthday party. Although I'd previously invited my mother, I was hoping she didn't turn up – but she did. I remember being excited at the start of my party, especially when my younger cousins told me how inspired and proud they were of me. They also said that if I could go to Uni and get my degree then so can they. This really made my night and I felt everything was worth it to hear these words from my cousins. When I saw my mother, I drank and smoke myself until I was numb. I don't remember much after that. The next day I was told how I was all over the floor, dancing crazily lol.

Friends

Throughout this stage of my life, there are a few people that had been tremendous in helping me night and day, such as Teni, Leah, Vivian, Cherina, Sarah, Naomi and my sister Joy. I want to take this opportunity to thank them so much for their love, care and support.

CHAPTER FOUR

Overcoming Challenges

Challenges

Needless to say, throughout my journey from childhood into adolescent, I'd been through many tough and extreme challenges. From that initial day in Jamaica when Uncle Benny molested me at five years old; Ken's ongoing sexual abuse, physically abused, and neglect at home; drug rape; watching my mother being violently abused; immigrating to the UK; drugs, sex and crime lifestyle, to being groomed by my one of my teachers at Lambeth College, and everything else in between.

Some of the most common questions I get asked are: "how did you overcome all those challenges?" "How did you get from where you were to where you are now?" "How can you really get over all these horrible things that's happened to you?" and "Could you truly be happy?" Can you show me how to do it too?

Since breaking my silence, I've consciously being on this ongoing journey of personal growth and success. I'm confident that many people can identify with most, if not all parts of my story. I'm no longer afraid to open up and be vulnerable. I no longer believe that it's my fault or that I'm alone. Each time I share my story, I gain new insights about myself as well as inspire many others.

I've found that many people (women and men) engage with my story because they or someone they know have had similar experiences, or they may connect from an angle of experiencing other serious types of challenges such as running a marathon, buying a home for the first time, getting married, "coming out" as being gay, starting a new career, making a big financial investment, standing up to your parents or facing another type of fearful challenge.

The main thing here is challenges vary. Our capacity to effectively deal with specific challenges varies too, depending on many factors including our general view of challenges as a whole.

Some of the key factors to overcoming challenges are:

1. Our individual definition and perception of challenges as a whole
2. How and when we acknowledge challenges
3. How we perceive the importance or unimportance of challenges
4. Our strategies in place to deal with individual challenging situations

I'll go through each of these below as I draw upon specific parts of my story, taking you on the journey of how I got to where I am now.

How do you define challenges?

I define a challenge as <u>any</u> situation that feels tough for ME to deal with. According to the Oxford dictionary, a challenge is:

> "something that needs great mental or physical effort in order to be done successfully and therefore tests a person's ability."

The extreme challenges that victims of abuse and violence are usually faced with, do tend to cause severe strain on their mental and physical abilities to deal with their experiences – especially when children are involved. From experiencing the actual act(s) of abuse and/or violence to overcoming its deep-rooted impacts, victims are usually left to deal with some of the toughest challenges as a result of these experiences. Abuse and violence are some of the most challenging situations any of us will ever have to face in our lifetime.

> "The deeper the challenge, the greater the opportunity to grow"
>
> ***Lioness Tamar***

How do you perceive challenges?

Growing up, I'd always seen 'challenging times' as a negative thing. Like something happening to me, outside of my control, for one reason or another. I usually put it down to 'lack'. For example, lack of money is why my mother turned back at the ***crossroad*** which later resulted in many more extreme challenges happening to her and her children. Also, although I often recognized my mother's strength, I thought she 'lacked' courage and that's why she put up with such abusive behavior from her partner(s). I know differently now, in that my mother IS the most courageous woman I know. I only realised this from viewing my challenges from different angels instead of sticking to the only version I knew in my childhood. But acknowledging how my childself viewed those challenges, give me deeper context to understanding my challenges overall from a 360 viewpoint. By doing so, I'm able to identify negative thought patterns that governed the way I think, feel and respond to my challenges.

To create sustainable change, it's important to understand the way we perceive the very thing we're trying to change. One way of doing so is to question your thoughts on the surface – dig below the surface to understand why you think, say or do the things you do. You're likely to find reasons associated with past events. You can then make a more informed decision whether any, some or all of those views still serve your purpose. If not, you can choose to change or completely let go of them. At the very least, you'll have a better understanding as to why you perceive certain things the way you do.

I'm not saying it's easy to dig deep within ourselves, but it's so worth it. You're worth it and I'm worth it too. The aim is to reach a more balanced place of being in terms of how we see challenges as a whole. From this angle, we become more likely to want to address the issue, as we claim back more of our power which give us greater inner strength to deal with the challenge.

I had to come to terms with my truth, which is that challenges help me to grow. When I reflected back on some of my best achievements, it probably wouldn't have happened but for the challenge behind the situation which tested my abilities and created new pathways within my mind. For example, but for the challenges around my UK status creating barriers for me to go to University, I wouldn't have been interested to help my family sort out our legal paperwork. What did I know? My mother was dealing with it! I had no need to worry myself about such things, besides I wouldn't have known the first thing to do! Nor would I have wanted to seek help as it involved openly disclosing our situation to officials and risked being sent back home. However, faced with the possibility of not being able to go to University and realised my potentials, after coming so far - opened up new pathways which led me on a journey to establishing my family and I permanent UK status. And as a result of this, new opportunities for growth have unfolded in abundance (and are still unfolding).

I can confidently say that challenges are a natural way of life. They're not here to keep us down, although when we're in deep distress, it completely feels that way. I now realize that this just means we weren't prepared for that challenge which can definitely be worked on, using ***The Lioness Way*** approach below. It's like walking into a battlefield – without the necessary protection, we have to be grateful that we made it out alive in the first place! When we are equipped with the right gear, we not only become masters of fighting these battles, we can also teach others how to become masters too.

How important are challenges?

Without challenges, what would our lives be like? I'm asking this question after I can now see the importance of challenges in my life.

I used to think that my life would be so much happier if I didn't have what I called "a hard life". I dreamed of the day I could leave my hard life behind and sit back to enjoy a much easier one. I didn't like hearing about other people's struggles because it reinforced to me the saying, "life is hard!" I thought MY life should be different, and it could be - once I had 'this', or 'that, which usually referred to some form of material things such as money or a big house. I believed I was entitled to it too, after the childhood I've had, but little did I know that no one owed me anything and it was MY responsibility to create the life I wanted. Instead I felt let down and misunderstood each time my life got harder and I got angrier with everything and everyone around me which is why I got into so many fights!

Essentially, I thought the world should put up with my negative behaviour and I used my challenges as excuses for my behaviour. I didn't think or care about my mother's or other peoples' challenges, how they may be coping or how my actions may be making it worse for them. It never crossed my mind how my actions could be making it worse for myself. I'd even feel very insulted and get angry if someone had suggested so. I just wanted better for myself (and my friends) but I didn't know how, when or where to get it. When I wasn't fighting my way through the walls, I was cheating by either stealing or tricking people so I could get what I thought I deserved.

I thought I was dealt "a bad hand" to begin this life and I was being tested or punished in some ways, but with enough money and other material things, the walls of my challenges would be removed from my life. That was MY aim – to remove challenges from my life so I could live "happily ever after"; just like I'd seen in the movies. When I didn't verbalize this, I just internalise it.

The older I got, the more I heard about famous rich stars and celebrities who seemed to have everything they needed, yet many of them were deeply unhappy. They spent a lot of money in therapy, or buying drugs, alcohol and other forms of mechanisms to cope through their unhappiness. Sometimes when I see their pictures in the media, I thought they either look like me or worse! We hear about them committing suicide, or having various mental health challenges. It was then that I realized that having all the money you want, doesn't prevent you from going through challenges, nor does it stop you from reacting negatively to them.

After unsuccessfully trying to buy, hide or run away from my challenges; or trying to block them out, pretending like they're not happening; or fight my way through, I started to ask myself some different kind of questions:

- What's the purpose of my challenges?
- Why are they important to me?

My son used to listen to a children's song on Youtube called '33 Positive Affirmations for Kids Self Esteem' and it says:

"I welcome challenges. Challenges helps me grow!"

Reflecting on this after hearing it over and over, I remember another statement I used to hear as a child.

"What doesn't kill you makes you stronger."

I can remember hearing this statement from those around me as well as in various songs. At the time, I'd hoped my challenges didn't kill me and now, I'm so glad they've made me the strongest I could possibly be.

I believe these 'statements' were teaching us about the importance of challenges. And it's not about putting us down or making us unhappy, although it's very easy to see it that way. I firmly believe now that by working through our challenges, we develop a stronger mental and emotional resilience, increased capacity of problem-solving, a clearer understanding of ourselves and what we do want.

Take for example, standing up to our parents. We may feel like we don't want to do that which they want us to do. But it can take a lot of courage and determination to overcome the fear and default programming that tells us "we can't.. challenge our parents". If we don't, we could be allowing them to control our entire adult lives, leading to deep unhappiness. However, by facing the situation, our aim is to get to a place where we can freely make our own decisions! Although it can be very challenging to achieve, when we fulfill these desires i.e. obtain freedom from our parents, we sometimes reflect and realized it was all worth it. Sometimes, it may involve not being in the same vicinity as our parents for a while, or other creative ways set and enforce our boundaries. One thing for sure is that we grow through the process and gain more clarity and insight about who we really are and what we're capable of.

Another thing to be mindful of is we're all on our own journey, and at different paces in our journey; and so, our challenges usually reflect back to us where we are, as opposed to where we thought we were. It's important to know where you are in relationship to where you want to be. Knowing this should help us embrace challenges and the wisdom they unfold in us; as opposed to comparing ourselves to others or getting too distracted in the negative emotions of challenges.

When to acknowledge challenges

Up to this point we've defined challenges, address our perception of challenges as well as the importance of challenges. We also need to know how to deal with challenges but before we discuss my 5-step process to overcoming challenges ***The Lioness Way***, let's find out when's to best time to acknowledge our challenges.

Have you ever heard the saying: "Don't wait for the roof to come crashing down before you fix it!?" In this context, the roof represents a big challenge. It's likely to have had many leaks before it fell down. How do we respond to leaks (i.e. early signs)?

Generally, most of us get a plaster and patch it up. This is especially the case with modern society where ease, convenience and a quick fix are prioritized. We also don't usually address what we can't see i.e. the bigger picture as to why the roof is leaking. This could be because we underestimated the problem; lack of prioritizing an appropriate solution; maybe we were following other people; or the length of time and cost it would take to fix it can be really stressful. By putting a strong enough plaster over it, we stopped the leak "without the hassle and additional cost". At this point, we're happy that the inconvenience and problem seemed to have gone away even if it's just temporary. We continue through our daily lives oblivious of the bigger problem building up behind the plaster. When the second leak occurred, we repeat the same process because of the results we achieved from patching up the first leak. We continue the same process over and over again for the fourth, fifth and all the other leaks that occurred before the roof finally collapsed. Then one day, we realized that our roof is full of plasters and patches! At this point, there seems to be a lot more physical evidence that there could potentially be a bigger problem. Now it's not as easy to ignore it. However, what we fail to realize in these situations, is that by the time the problem becomes that obvious, it would've required urgent action (and in some cases, no amount of action can prevent the inevitable at this point as it maybe way too late). But as we're just becoming aware of a possibly bigger problem, we may not see it for what it truly is. And so, even with the best intentions, the roof still came crashing down.

This roof analogy is similar to our challenges. Before a challenge unfolds with full effect on our lives, there are usually what we call, 'early signs'. These early signs are normally picked up by us on a spiritual level first, before they manifest into our physical reality. They are usually things we may not be able to see, understand or explain clearly, unless we become aware and focus our attention to it. We get a sense of these earlier signs through our intuition, feelings, emotions, visions and hearing. When we ignore them, block them out or pretend like they're not happening, they don't just go away. Instead they fester and grow into much bigger problems that can completely disrupt an area of our life or our entire lives.

Early signs: domestic abuse

Domestic abuse and violence is abuse power and control. It's extra important to be able to spot the signs from early. Doing so could alert you to act fast, protecting yourself, your children or a loved one from potential harm. Also when we receive the right support at an earlier stage of experiencing domestic abuse or child abuse, it help us to rebuild our lives more effectively – giving us a better chance of living a happy and fulfilling life.

It's not always easy to spot abuse though, as many people tend to look for physical violence as evidence of a problem. But signs of this level of violence usually means more complex and deeper issues which can still be easily hidden. That's why I feel it's essential to highlight some of the earlier signs below.

Signs that a relationship is unhealthy usually comes before the violence, such as any indication a person is being controlled or scared of what their partner may think, say or do. If you feel unsafe or recognise any of the signs below. Take action. See the back of this book for organisations that maybe able to help, or search online for other resources that maybe more local to you.

Here are 10 early signs of unhealthy relationships which create the platform for toxic and unhealthy relationships:

1. "You're becoming a lot more critical of yourself — thinking you are stupid or fat or very lucky to have a partner.
2. You give up on your own opinions and think your partner is right about everything.
3. You're feeling more stressed or worried all the time; you feel nauseous or have bad butterflies. Sometimes stress can also stop us eating and sleeping properly, or cause us to have headaches.
4. You have that 'dreaded' feeling more often (especially when you're around them).
5. You're scared of how your partner will react to a situation.
6. You avoid saying something because you don't want to upset your partner.
7. You feel scared when your partner is angry because you can't predict their behaviour.
8. You're feeling a pressure to change who you are or move the relationship further than you want to.
9. You feel like you're walking on eggshells.
10. You're staying in more and seeing less of family and friends to avoid arguments with your partner." [35]

It's important to note the definition of domestic abuse is not just restricted to partners or ex-partners, but especially in the Black and Minority Ethnic (BAME) community, it may also include family members and carers. [36]

---

35 https://www.victimsupport.org.uk

36 https://www.womensaid.org.uk/information-support/what-is-domestic-abuse/

Emotional and Mental abuse

The most common forms of abuse I'm aware of are emotional [37] and mental abuse [38]. Any of the above examples could cause this. For example, "feeling like you're walking on egg shelves" makes you second guest everything, and sometimes you may act like you don't know what you're doing when in fact, you're trying not to upset them or make things worse. But they still find a way to flip it around on you to make you feel like you're going mad and call you names like "stupid" or "idiot" or some other insulting words. No one can see how they've consumed your mind and how distressing this can be.

Emotional and mental/ psychological abuse as well as cohesive control can be some of the most challenging forms of abuse for its victims to accept and come to terms that they're been affected in this way; as well as having the ability to clearly express themselves and for others to take them seriously. This is particularly challenging in certain African, Caribbean and other minority ethnic communities. Because of these and many other barriers, early signs of 'non-physical' abuse tends to get brushed under the carpet, sadly until it gets more serious.

In some cases, we've seen the victims end up acting so much out of character like "Sally Challen who's sentence was recently overturned.. allowing her to walk freely ..after murdering her husband after years of being controlled and humiliated by him. He bullied and belittled her, controlled their money and who she was friends with, not allowing her to socialise without him. But, whilst

---

37 https://www.relate.org.uk/relationship-help/help-relationships/arguing-and-conflict/what-emotional-abuse

38 "Psychological abuse involves a person's attempts to frighten, control, or isolate you. It's in the abuser's words and actions, as well as their persistence in these behaviors:" https://www.healthline.com/health/signs-of-mental-abuse

he forced strict restrictions on her behavior, he himself, would flaunt his money, have numerous affairs and visit brothels. If she challenged him, he would turn it back on her and make her feel she was going mad. Although Sally did manage at one point to leave Richard, even starting divorce proceedings, she was so emotionally dependent on him that she soon returned.. The final straw was when he sent Sally out in the rain to get his lunch so that he could phone a woman he had been planning to meet from a dating agency. Sally returned suspicious and challenged him, he commanded her not to question him and she struck him repeatedly with a hammer." [39]

I've also seen from my mother's situation of being in long term domestic violence relationships that long after leaving the environment where the physical violence took place, the emotional and mental impact was much more long lasting to heal, leaving her vulnerable to repeated victimisation.

For these cases and many other stories, it's more essential now than ever before for each of us to get educated on the early signs of domestic abuse/toxic relationships and what to do about it. Children should also learn this information too both at schools and at homes so we don't wait until we're caught up in unhealthy relationships and then having to figure it all out on our own. By then, it tends to get worse before it gets better.

39 https://www.justiceforwomen.org.uk/sally-challen-appeal

Early signs: child abuse

Common signs

Some common signs that there may be something concerning happening in a child's life include:

- unexplained changes in behaviour or personality
- becoming withdrawn
- seeming anxious
- becoming uncharacteristically aggressive
- lacks social skills and has few friends, if any
- poor bond or relationship with a parent
- knowledge of adult issues inappropriate for their age
- running away or going missing
- always choosing to wear clothes which cover their body.

When it comes to child abuse, the signs to look out for are slightly different and more complex because these same signs can be an indication of other things happening in a child's life. If you spot any of the signs, contact the NSPCC who will be able to guide you further. [40]

As a child who experienced sexual abuse at home, I displayed all of the above signs except physically running away which I did later in my teens. I also peed my bed throughout my childhood years which made me think even less of myself, and I felt extreme belly pain that required medical attention.

These were key signs that something wasn't quite right with me, and therefore it needed further investigation, but as in many other cases, they get missed or overlooked, for one reason or another.

Early signs: generational abuse

It can be even more complex to spot early signs where there has been a cycle of abuse across generations within a family. The

40 https://www.nspcc.org.uk/what-is-child-abuse/spotting-signs-child-abuse/

problem didn't start with the last known person in the family who became a victim. No, it started way before then. We know that female survivors of domestic abuse or child abuse are more vulnerable to revictimisation. We also know that without the right support, survivors' children are at high risk to becoming victims or perpetrators themselves. [41] Although most domestic abuse organisations don't acknowledge that women from certain ethnic cultures are more at risk of abuse or violence; some do state that, "..women from Black, Asian or minority ethnic (BAME) communities are likely to face additional barriers to receiving the help that they need." [42] "Research on Intergenerational Continuity of Violence and Adversity finds that individuals who experience abuse, neglect, or other forms of childhood adversity are more likely than are nonexposed individuals to have children who go on to have similar adverse childhood experiences." [43] Considering the extreme and horrific violence and abuse the Black community in particular, experienced during slavery - without access to the right support to heal and rebuild our lives - I believe this increases the risk of revictimisation amongst females (and males) survivors of slave descendants. However, because of the silence and stigma still associated with domestic abuse, child abuse and sexual violence (amongst other things) in our community, it creates many more layers and barriers to identifying signs from earlier on. Instead learnt behaviour - at its very core - becomes the norms and is still heavily influencing our modern-day approach to these challenges.

When these issues are not being addressed properly, or they're swept under the carpet, or victims and survivors are not seen to be

41 https://www.refuge.org.uk/get-help-now/support-for-women/what-about-my-children/

42 https://www.womensaid.org.uk/the-survivors-handbook/women-from-bme-communities/

43 https://www.ncbi.nlm.nih.gov/pmc/articles/PMC6085055/

listened to or supported – it creates the foundation for the cycle to continue into future generations. Before you know it, most, if not all mothers of a specific bloodlines, end up experiencing some form of abuse/violence, as a common thing.

For example, a woman who had previously experienced childhood sexual abuse but didn't receive the support she needed to heal – is likely to still being affected by it when she later becomes a mother. Her ability to spot early signs or create healthy bonds and boundaries may've still been impaired somewhat, depending on how much her experiences had affected her. This could then lead to her making unwise decisions about her chosen partners or even who to trust around her child. Without knowing it, she could be facilitating the environment for what happened to her, to happen to her child too [44] (whether it's a boy or girl child). And so, the cycle continues.

If you've experienced abuse or violence, like me, you've clearly been through some challenging situations. It's important you know it's not your fault, help is available and you can grow past the negative impact it's caused you. I believe the earlier in your life this is picked up and start to be dealt with appropriately, the easier it will be on your mental and emotional state throughout the rest of your life. And so, the quicker you will be able to grow through it.

If your child has also become a victim, it's important that they feel they can talk to you about this. If you've experienced similar emotions in your life (whether abuse related or not), it's ok to adapt your experiences to the child's appropriate age and share it with your child. This will help them understand more clearly how to deal with it, through the ways you may or may not have dealt with yours. I believe it's important they see and hear you talk about your

44 https://link.springer.com/article/10.1007/s00737-016-0708-3

experiences as that gives them the permission and validation they need to release their pain. By doing so, they may not need to look elsewhere for validation as not everyone will have your child's best interests at heart.

"Children live what they learn."

In summary, it's important for us to spot challenges earlier i.e. before the roof crashes. I believe that to do this, we must connect deeper with our spiritual side. Think back to when a problem unfolded and you can remember telling yourself, "I knew it!" You may've heard a voice in your mind telling you about it, or you just had a feeling or some other sign. In Jamaica, we often say "mi spirit tell mi yuh nuh", or "mi spirit nuh tek dem." This indicates the communication between our spirit and our physical selves. Our issue as a people is, we've become too disconnected from our spiritual self and therefore relying heavily on physical evidence manifestation before we give it our full attention. But by then, it's usually too late.

How do we spot a challenge from earlier on? As I believe we're all spiritual beings in physical bodies, I suggest the most authentic way is to re-connect with our spiritual selves through meditation, deep breathing and affirmative prayer. This allows ourselves to be guided by the spirit.

By doing so, you will receive all the benefits from your challenges including growth, expansion, insight and clarity. And yet challenges won't have as much impact on your mental and emotional state. Without realizing it, we're not only making huge improvements in our lives, we're also redefining challenges and showing our future generations how to deal with it more effectively.

I trust that we're now seeing challenges through similar lenses:

1. Like me, we all go through tough situations that tests our abilities and requires great mental or physical effort in order to complete it successfully.
2. The way we perceived our challenges usually defines whether we openly face them as they're happening or we try (one way or the other) to avoid them until the roof finally crashes leaving us extra vulnerable in the midst of the storm.
3. These situations are not hear to "give us a hard life" but instead, they teach us about ourselves and our personal power to achieve the things we desire. They bless us with deep insight and wisdom that shows us where we are in relation to where we want to be.
4. Spotting the early signs of a challenge can put us in the best position to deal with it. Some challenges may be more complex to spot and handle. However, as spiritual beings, reconnecting with our Higher Power will put us in the best possible position to identify challenges from earlier on, and with the effective strategies discussed below in '***The Lioness Way***', we'll also know the best way to deal with them.

Strategies: 5 Steps to Overcoming Challenges '*The Lioness Way*'

Now that we've set the parameters for understanding our challenges, I'll continue with my proven blueprint: 5-Steps to Overcoming Challenges '***The Lioness Way***', which is based upon Law of Attraction's principles.

Recovering from the biggest trigger to date, I realised that fighting was my defaulted mechanisms in dealing with tough challenges. But

I had to accept I couldn't fight my way through everything. I needed new tools, new mechanisms and new strategies.

I remember asking my therapist how can I protect myself from falling so deeply again. She explained to me about various tools and strategies I could use to connect deeper with my spirit and so I'll benefit from stronger protection. I came home that day and looked up some of these including meditation, deep breathing and mindfulness. The more I practiced these tools, the more I started to learn about even more tools that were useful too including positive mindset, gratitude and affirmations.

Having explored various of these tools, I used the ones I enjoyed most to create a daily routine which I practiced everyday, and still do to date. This part of my journey was very exciting, like I was finding myself for the first time or painting a new picture on a blank canvas. I was able to realise what worked or didn't work for me. I'm honoured and committed myself to what was working whilst releasing what no longer served me including negative habits, people and experiences. I later received a vision about my life which has been my guiding force to this point.

Through it all, I've been through many other challenges, however I now experience them differently. Through mindfulness, meditation, reflection and journaling, I've been able to process and articulate the steps that I was been guided to follow, each time a challenge came my way. I used this process to create my blueprint: 5 steps to Overcoming Challenges '***The Lioness Way***'. I've since used '***The Lioness Way***' to empower many other women and girls to rebuild their lives both at **The Lioness Circle**'s domestic abuse and sexual violence programmes as well as my own private clients.

Those who knows me, knows how challenging my journey has been, leaving me feeling helpless time after time! However from where I am today I can confidently say, we do have a choice how we respond to our challenges, no matter how tough they may seem. We can decide to keep fighting, (like I was), trying to block it out OR face it (before it gets triggered). Facing it is the first step of my 5 Steps to Overcoming Challenges '***The Lioness Way***'.

Step 1: Facing it

"Explore the problem without judgement – in order to gain a better understanding of how you deal with similar challenges."

Lioness Tamar

- Tip: Step 1 is usually the most challenging part of the 5 steps and so, may require much of your time to fully grow through. If you're not used to understanding your thoughts and emotions, you may find it easier reflecting on a challenge you've already overcome, rather than one that is currently active in your vibrations.
- **Warning**: this activity may bring back some painful memories. Self care is very important when doing any kind of work on ourselves. So, please take care and reach out for help if you need it. I've put some additional resources at the back of this book which you may find useful. Alternatively, you can also

download a free copy of my ebook, 'The Lioness Guide to Self Care' directly from: www.lionesstamar.com.

- Are you ready? Thinking of a challenging situation, ask yourself,
  "How did I react to that situation, in terms of my thoughts, emotions, habits and actions? How do I usually deal with these kind of challenging situations? Why do I respond in this way?" "What's my default pattern of response?"
  Doing this will give you great insight into your default response system when it come to challenges as well as what's at the core of your response programming. Before we can create change, we must first identify what is it we're trying to change.
- Once you become more comfortable dealing with your thoughts and emotions, you can start to identify your default response programme, as they're happening in the moment and be able to redirect yourself into thinking and doing more pleasing thoughts and things.

See below for my own reflection on facing my biggest challenge to date – 'The Breaking Silence' period. I've had to do this kind of reflection on many occasions in order to create the change, I wanted to see within myself. Each time I reflected back, it was for a different purpose and I've always learnt something new about myself or how I dealt with things.

My thoughts

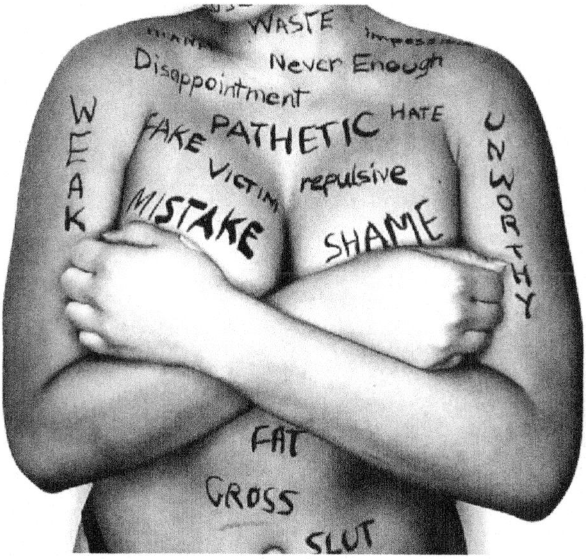

Sitting in my Criminal Law class that day at Uni, there were so many voices going wild in my mind. They were screaming and shouting at me that everyone was going to find out what had happened. I thought they would all blame me and call me names, just like they did back in Heskit when they found out about my rape allegation.

I remember blaming myself saying, "This is all your fault for not preparing for this class like you'd normally do. You've come so far, for what? You're not cut out for this. You can't do this. Who are you trying to fool?"

I wanted to run and escape but I couldn't. Part of me felt stuck to the chair whilst my thoughts reinforced to me that it was safer to stay seated. So, I surrendered to my mental battle. I paid the price of "containing my secret" by staying seated. I was at the mercy of these horrific thoughts, flashbacks and screaming sounds, with a picture of a monstrous version of Ken's face, close up to mine, breaking me down even more. It was unlike anything I'd ever experience!

I never wanted to feel like this again. I used mindfulness to be more aware of the general chitter chatter that went on in my mind each day. I'd then journaled to process my thoughts and gain a clearer understanding. Afterwhich, I'd write positive affirmations on cards and post them up on my wall where I could see them throughout the day. For example, "I am strong." "I am phenomenal." "I am love." I also used my phone alarm to remind me different empowering statements at different interval throughout the day.

For example, at 2pm, my phone alarm would go off, and when I looked at it, it said "You are worthy". Another example is at 10pm, my alarm goes off again. This time it says, "I forgive you for all the mistakes you made today".

These processes were all helping me to reprogram my mind. Whenever a challenge occurred, the mind would automatically go back to its negative self-critique ways but the more I was able to catch these thoughts in the moment, the more impact I could have in changing them from negative to positive. And of course, the more I did this over time, the more I heard my thoughts automatically changing themselves from negative to positive without much conscious effort.

My feelings/emotions

In the midst of the trigger, I felt many mixed emotions. For example, I felt anxious, scared and worried that my past was catching up on me. I felt angry that the world I'd worked so hard to build was about to crumble. I felt powerless and alone that 'my secrets were out of the bag' which also made me felt tense, embarrassed and ashamed. It was confusing how quickly and suddenly this was all happening - like someone had set me up and was secretly having a laugh at my expense – problem is, it wasn't funny. When I wanted to get up and leave my seat, I felt stuck, and by the time I got up, I was so angry, I wanted to punch something or someone.

I also remember feeling some intense pain in my chest like someone was pulling out my rib cage. The pain stayed there for a while before it disappeared to other parts of my body. I've now identified this pain. It's linked to the stress and anxiety from the panic attack I was clearly experiencing. It started with my head pounding, then my chest, then it moved down into my hips and waist area where it stayed for a long time afterwards. I became very stiff and tense in my body, causing me neck and back pain.

Also, whenever I'd try to dance, I'd look and feel really stiff without understanding why. For a long time I was embarrassed and felt jealous of everyone else who could freely move their body. I also had social anxiety dancing around people or going out partying with my friends as I thought everyone would stare at me and laugh when they realise I couldn't dance. I dreaded this feeling. This made me not go out sometimes or I'd stay in a corner with huge anxiety, away from the spotlight, when I do go out. I'd rely on alcohol and weed to calm my nerves before sometimes attempting to dance. But sometimes this backfired leaving me feeling more paranoid and tense. I felt so let down when it came to dancing. In Jamaica, girls are expected to know how to do two main things, that's cooking and dancing. At the time I couldn't do much of either!

However, understanding what's at the root of my body being so tense and stiff has helped me to take extra care of myself such as having long baths regularly, attended various yoga classes, incorporate stretches in my morning routine and having fun dancing at home. I've also taken various beginners dance classes to loosen up my body more including the one I'm currently doing at **The Lioness Circle**. I visit the spa every week with some of the other Lionesses and I recently completed a 30 days gut cleanser and detox programme, facilitated by Heaven Africa.

My actions

My initial reaction was to freeze, flight and fight. When I finally came to, I heard the lecturer said, "This class has been dismissed." At that point, my mind told me it was safe to go. I quickly jumped up from my seat without saying a word and escaped through the door. I ran down the corridor as fast as I could. I was so angry, my fingers wrapped in a tight fist. My heart racing whilst breathing fast through my mouth. I'm so glad no one tried to stop me because I didn't know what I was capable of doing. My head was pounding. I couldn't hold back the tears. The faster I ran, the more I cried.

Exploring my reaction, I realised I'd experienced all three of our body's automatic response to serious threat or harm. At first, I froze (by feeling stuck), then fight (through crying, firmed fist and feeling angry), and then flight (by running away). [45]

45 https://trauma-recovery.ca/impact-effects-of-trauma/fight-flight-freezeresponses

It was a very critical moment for me, in many ways than I'd realised. Reflecting on it gave me further clarity about the ways I'd responded to perceived threats.

If you'd asked me, I would've said my main reaction was to get angry and wanting to fight straight away. However, after that day, I realised I do tend to feel stuck at first, and then I'd fight my way through. I also realised I'd been running away mentally all my life and so, it's only natural for me to physically run away from the problem too. If I'm to be honest, I usually try to escape uncomfortable situations to finding somewhere more relaxing. This could've been at a guy's house or hanging out with my friends. I'd become so oblivious to my process that I was unconscious of the initial part of feeling stuck or running away afterwards. I wonder how many of you can relate to this?

However now I knew this vital piece of information, I could use it to manage my responses better. It was important to me to not beat up on myself for when I felt I'd lost control. Instead, I'd redirected my focus on things that calmed me down such as deep and slow breathing and my 'happy place', before I completely loose my temper.

Another action I noticed I did differently at the time, was the fact I ran to find a counsellor for the very first time instead of going home to my usual drugs, alcohol and binge eating habits. This made me see myself and my capabilities in a different light. For the first time, I consciously became aware that I could trust myself to do the right thing for me, even in the darkest moments. This was huge! It showed me my courage and strength. It helped to build my confidence, self-esteem and trust within myself. I was really starting to understand who I really am.

I never wanted to feel like how I'd felt in the midst of that trigger again. I've since spent much time in therapy and educating myself around my thoughts and emotions; how to manage them and how I can make them work better for me. I've completed CBT (Cognitive Behavioural Therapy) and emotional intelligence online courses. I also use daily breathing exercises to free up my mind and body, and raise my vibrations to higher and more positive levels. I can now confidently say I have a better understanding of my thoughts patterns which impact my emotions and perceptions, and together, they control the way I behave. My behaviour also reinforces them too. To change the way I behave, I understood that it was important to first change my thoughts, and feelings and perceptions.

My defaulted pattern of response

By doing the above work I started to see a pattern in how I'd been dealing with challenging situations. It would start with familiar thoughts and emotions around feeling stuck, then I'd want to fight my way through things. Even when I felt scared or anxious, I'd still want to fight. I don't usually run from a fight unless in extreme cases like that night in Brixton when my life flashed in front of me, or when those Peckham girls were throwing broken bottles after my friends and I.

Any left over debris usually got swept under the carpet as I'd run for safety and use my old habits to make myself feel better, although I often ended up feeling worse deep inside. After I'd calm down, I'd feel like the victim; reinforced by my thoughts that someone was doing 'it' to me.

I'd blamed myself and others for adding to my existing baggage. I thought people didn't like me and that's why they did hurtful things to me.

I now recognized that this toxic pattern of reacting to challenges was as a result of negative programming from my early years of abuse and violence. A lot of what I experienced back then transformed into internalized anger. I was helpless to stopping the abuse or violence. I didn't have anyone to speak to about it and so, I had to find ways to make myself feel better about coping in it. This became my default way of dealing with challenges. In fact, I wasn't really dealing with the challenge itself and so, the cycle continued which showed up in different forms, times and places.

I remember that I also had speech impediment (stammer) as a child, which, combined with the forced silence of child abuse, I felt disabled when it came to talking about my problems. Instead, I would more easily get overwhelmed in the emotions, curse and shout, or in some cases, I'd completely ignore the issue by blocking it out where I felt my actions wouldn't make much difference.

This knowledge enlightened my mind and changed a lot within me. By getting to the core and facing my real challenges, one of the things it changed, was that I acknowledged, accepted and validated the hurt and pain as part of my many experiences, which weren't all sad. By doing this, I was getting ready to 'Let Go' of the hurt and pain, which is Step 2 of my 5 Steps to Overcoming Challenges '***The Lioness Way***'

Before I move on to Step 2, I know some people may not be as comfortable with the word 'acceptance' in the context of hurt and pain. For this reason, I'll expand further.

"Acceptance is acknowledging what's already happened; approval is consenting to more of it in the future. To accept that the person you're in a committed relationship with has a side to

him that causes harm to you doesn't mean that you're okay with it or want it to keep happening." [46]

I used to think that because I "rolled over and allowed them" to do whatever they wanted to me, that meant I'd accepted it. But that couldn't be further away from the truth!

I remember working in a previous employment, one of my managers taught me that a huge part of problem-solving is assessing each situation for that which is within one's control and that which isn't. It's not within my control to change the past. I can only accept that its already happened, and so, I can choose to learn from it and move on. Besides I've already lived life on the other side of not wanting to accept this and so I've found myself in much more challenging situations which doesn't serve my purpose.

For some people who hasn't yet accepted their past, they may find themselves in various toxic cycles and having the same conversations with different people in different situations. It's like there are unconsciously stuck on a replay. I'm sure we all know at least one person like that. If not, it's probably ourselves. If this sound like it could be you, it's ok, you're not alone. Help is available. You could continue practicing my 5 Steps to Overcoming Challenges '***The Lioness Way***'. Or if you finds it too challenging, contact your doctor for counselling support as well as seek out support networks like my Lioness Circle where you could access free mentoring, coaching and peer to peer support, amongst other things.

The bottom line is that acceptance is a natural part of acknowledging what's already happened, in order to let go and conscious-

46 https://www.psychologytoday.com/us/blog/mindfully-present-fullyalive/201711/the-inescapable-importance-acceptance

ly decide how you now want things to be. According to Abraham Hicks,

"Contrast cause you to know what you don't want in order to know what you do."

If you're ready and able to face your 'contrast' i.e. challenges, and allow yourself to go through the uncomfortable feelings and the knowledge of self that 'Step 1' may disrupt within you, you'll become more aware of what do you want. You won't be able stay where you were when you first started. Like me, you'll not only desire better for yourself, you'll start to see a possibly path of achieving it. You'll come to understand the best way forward is by accepting it, then letting it go.

By facing and accepting my past experiences, I validated my own hurt and pain; and gave myself permission to change my actions. I thanked my toxic default patterns for serving its purpose, and acknowledged it was no longer required.

STEP 2: Letting Go

"*Let go of the hurt and pain; and claim your power back!*"

Lioness Tamar

- Reflecting on the lessons learnt in Step 1, write a letter to all the people you think have hurt you. Tell them how their words and actions made you feel. Let them know you're taking back control over your life now.
- Fold the letter away you, then soak it in water or burn it (in a safe place) as a symbol of letting go.
- As you do this, affirm to yourself, "I fully reclaim my power from these situations and release them from my mind, body and spirit!"
- Allow yourself to feel the difference inside which may include a feeling of rebirth, increased strength and possibilities. Revel in it. Journal about it. Talk to people around you that you know will encourage and lift you up even more.

We were born powerful Beings. It **IS** our birthright! No situation or circumstances, no matter how challenging, cannot change that. The only thing to consider is whether we're connected or disconnected from our inner power.

Think of yourself as a microwave and the electricity is your Power Source. Once you're plugged in, you can operate at full capacity.

When we feel stuck in a challenge, we tend to feel helpless. If we fail to identify and let go of the pain and hurt, we become unplugged and drift away from our Power Source.

If you're plugged out, you become dormant in that period. You'll still exist, but not really living or enjoying the true peace and happiness we came to experience.

Practicing this process of letting go is necessary to take you closer to who you really are. By doing so, you can spot challenges from earlier on and rise above them too. You'll be able to think and feel more clearly and independently of challenges or default patterns. This will put you in a much better position to receiving new ideas and solutions rather than remaining stuck and banging your head on the wall or pretending like it's not happening. You are the CEO of your life!

As CEO, you'll have the capacity to tailor your response to reflect the actual situation rather than allowing automatic default programming to control how your behaviour.

Have you notice how we sometimes react aggressively towards our children for simply reasons like them running in the house or jumping on the sofa? Have you felt victimized at work because you were told off for something you believed was trivial, e.g. like being 5 minutes late? Or have you reacted negatively to what you'd assumed someone meant without seeking clarification. Or maybe you stayed a relationship after someone had broken your trust over and over again?

Whatever examples we have of behaving disproportionately, the main thing here is we can break the cycle, by letting go of our deep-rooted pain, take back our power and embrace the life we truly desire.

Forgiveness

When we talk about 'letting go', other elements come into play too, such as forgiveness, surrender, freedom, and self-love. I once heard the saying that forgiveness is the key to inner peace and freedom. When we truly accept and forgive, we'll find it much easier to let go.

Coming from a Christian background, I only knew of forgiveness in the context that you have to forgive others to go to heaven. I thought forgiveness was something you just do. Like drinking water. Plus, I didn't really think I was doing it for me, except that it's a requirement of Heaven and I'll to go there if I just ticked this box that say "I forgive.." Everyone wanted to go to heaven but no one said what forgiveness was really about, at least not in a way that I understood it.

I thought that if I couldn't forgive people that's wronged me, then I wasn't "worthy" or "godly" enough. How I processed this was to try really hard to block things out. The more I was able to block it out and "forget", the more I thought I'd forgiven; until something triggered it all off, and all the hurt and pain would resurface. Forgetting is definitely not the same as forgiving as we're not truly letting go.

According to the Cambridge dictionary, forgiveness means,

'We stop blaming or being angry with someone for something they've done.' [47]

Whilst I agree that this definition is a benefit of forgiveness, it doesn't tell us how or why. You forgive others, not to go to heaven

---

47 https://www.google.com/amp/s/dictionary.cambridge.org/amp/english/ forgive

or for any other reward but to free yourself from the pain and hurt it brings holding onto it. You forgive to let go, because you love yourself and know you deserve more. I forgive because I know everything happens for a reason and there are lessons to be learnt in every season. Forgiveness is a process that happens overtime and should not be expected to be any other way.

I felt like I jumped some huge step forward when I chose to accept, forgive, let go and surrender! Something wonderful changed inside. For the first time, I consciously tapped into the power I always knew (deep down) I had. I'd already tasted it. For example, by passing my exams in Jamaica to go to Mannings High – the best High School in the area, after I was drug raped and still being sexually abused by my step dad; or when I came off the streets in my teenage years and went to college to redo my GCSE's and off to Universit, although I was being groomed by one of my teachers; or by leading the process into the unknown for my family and I to receive our permanent residency status in the UK; or even by being the first member of my family to attend University. I knew this inner power existed as part of who I am – I just didn't know until this moment, how to consciously tap into it.

My inner child was very wounded and had controlled my responses to what she'd perceived as potential threat. I healed her, built trust and boundaries between the adult and child in me. This allowed the child self to feel safe, releasing control to the adult self and now, they love playing together and having fun.

These processes worked wonders to help me feel alive from the inside. This was the first time in my life I was experiencing this level of happiness without any external factors or someone being my point of focus. I learnt so much about myself. I couldn't bare going back to how life was before. My commitment to self, to maintaining this good feeling, led me on the path of discovering even more new habits. I used these habits/tools to create the lifestyle I desired, plus, it was great for managing my mental and emotional wellbeing. It is because of the positive impact new habits have made on my self-healing as to why I put 'Creating New Habits' as Step 3. Some people may've already started creating new habits as part of their coping mechanisms or self-care tool to get them to this point. In fact, this is very good if that's you – continue building on those new habits. If you have not yet created any new habits, now is a great time to start!

STEP 3: Creating New Habits

"Out with the old, in with the new. Letting go of the things no longer serves us, make way for the things that do."

Lioness Tamar

- Take a deep breath, hold it for as long as you can. As you slowly exhale, feel the love, strength and power inside you.
- Stand in front of a mirror and repeat positive affirmations to yourself such as: "I am worthy", "I am happy", "Freedom is my birth right", "I am a co-creator", "I am creating my own destiny", and "I love me".
- Celebrate yourself and your journey so far. Be happy that you're on your way to thriving after experiencing some of the most extreme challenges. Allow yourself to revel in the knowing that you have the capacity to find your way back to your Source of

Power, with new growth, no matter the experience that may've disconnected you in the first place.
- From this new perspective, using visualisation techniques, focus on the life you want to live. The one you know you deserve (if money or time wasn't a problem). Write it down, draw it or paint it. Create a vision board using images and words to highlight your vision. Put it somewhere you can see it each morning you wake up. Look at it as many times as possible throughout the each day.

Now that you've let go of the old, it's time to focus on creating the new, life you want. Many people believe they have to put up with the cards they've been dealt, no matter how hard life gets.

Some people spend their lives repeating the same cycle, hoping that one day they'll be happy. Other people just do it out of obligations even if it clearly makes them unhappy like working in an unsatisfying job just to pay the bills or living the life someone else wants you to i.e their parents.

Albert Einstein said, "Doing the same thing, over and over, and expecting a different result is insanity." Abraham Hicks says, to be truly happy, you must practice the vibration of happiness now and the Laws of Attraction will bring more things in your reality to be happy about.

But some people may never have been told to put themselves first or understand what true happiness is about. I can certainly testify to this earlier in my life. We miss out on fun times and make excuses why. Some people who live to see old age, are full of remorse and regrets. They dream of having another chance to start over and do the things they actually wanted to do. Well, here is our second chance, what are we going to do with it?

It may help provide more clarity and empowerment if you think of your brain as the main control point of the body; it control things like your thoughts, feelings, perspective, movement, learning, memory as well as other less conscious things like digesting your food. Like any other computer, the brain can be reprogrammed, updated, and protected from infestation of things that do not serve you.

Understand that the way past experiences had impacted you, include default programming of the mind. This was necessary to help you cope during those challenging times. I believe the more extreme and traumatic the challenge, the deeper engrained the subconscious default programming. However, as you're no longer in those situations, you can now decide to reprogram the mind more consciously and intentionally to serve you where you are and where you want to be.

"Move the goalpost!" is a saying that's recently been going around in my head since hearing it from one of the Lionesses at **The Lioness Circle**. In Step 2, you already made the commitment to let go of past hurt and pain. To do so effectively, it's now important to actually move the goalposts by creating new programming to refocus the mind on what you want.

The tools points listed on the previous page can create one main habit. By exploring new habits like these, you are reprogramming the mind to become more open to transforming positive changes within you, in order to start attracting the life you want. At the very least, these activities may make you feel more valued and appreciated from within. They generated such good feeling thoughts and emotions within me, after a while, it was like being in a good mood all the time (more or less)!

Visualisation

One of my favourite tools is Visualisation which is, "any technique for creating images, diagrams, or animations to communicate a message." [48] "Visualisation techniques have been used by successful people to visualise their desired outcomes for ages." [49] "To succeed with visualisation, you must generate the same feelings and emotions that you would have if you had already accomplished your goals. Seeing the pictures in your mind is not enough – you have to show your brain which feelings it has to look out for. Envelop yourself in these wonderful positive emotions." [50]

One of my main visualisation technique is one from Lisa Nichols: 'How to Perform Visualisation Correctly'. It raised my vibrations instantly and gave me more context to my initial vision of seeing bright light surrounding me. The first time I listened to it, I cried like a baby. I felt every single word. It was like she was telling my story. Since then I have shared my childhood story in front of thousands of people at the Labour Party's Annual Conference 2019 in Brighton, UK. Many people in the audience thanked me; one woman never spoke, she just hugged me tightly and I saw others crying tears of happiness. It gave me a taste of what's coming and it definitely reminded me of Lisa's visualisation exercise that I love so much. As if that's not satisfying enough, when I posted the video clip of my speech on LinkedIn four months ago, Lisa Nichols commented on it, saying:

You can only imagine how elevated I felt to see this comment from Lisa, not only because she's such an inspirational siStar, but

---

48 https://en.m.wikipedia.org/wiki/Visualization_(graphics)

49 https://www.google.com/amp/s/www.jackcanfield.com/blog/visualize-and-affirm-your-desired-outcomes-a-step-by-step-guide/amp/

50 https://www.personal-development-planet.com/how-to-visualise.html

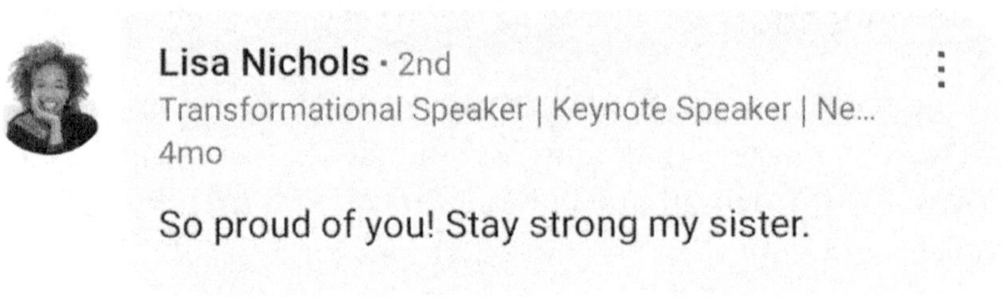

also because of the positive reinforcements and alignment of my desire it brings. I know this piece of unfoldment was part of its manifesting into my life. I've done the work in raising my vibrations through creating and practicing my new habits, and now the co-operative components are coming together to manifest my desires into my reality.

One time ago, I'd never think things like this was possible for people like me, more over to allow myself the opportunity of it actually happening. What I didn't know back then is if you can't think it or imagine it, it probably won't happen, because whatever we focus on that which we will receive.

However, having been doing the consistent work around reprogramming my mindset, it feels natural to me now that these opportunities are being attracted in my reality. I now know that I am worth it, and I deserve it, regardless of my background. And so do you too.

Self forgiveness

Another one of my positive habits was also inspired by Lisa Nichols. I get to forgive myself everyday for things I allowed to happen but in hindsight, I don't think they served my purpose well. By doing this, I release all negative energy including hurt and pain, shame and blame. Here's a typical example: standing in front of the mirror, looking into my eyes, I say:

"I Tamar forgive me for not putting myself first. Tamar, I forgive you for not putting you first."

Initially, it was very challenging coming to terms with some of these emotions behind the words. I cried a lot. I was starting to realise more and more how much I'd neglected myself and my wellbeing. This was less about blame or shame; and more about my commitment to forgiving myself and taking better care of me. This meant I was no longer going to allow certain things to happen to me again. I was making this decisions to stand up for me; to be there for me; and to put my needs first! This felt really empowering and helped to reinforce I can create positive changes from within.

As I've said before, there's an abundance of tools to access. Whichever ones work for you, it's important to practice them on a daily basis! Some of my daily tools are forgiveness, visualisation, meditation, affirmation, gratitude and journaling. Others, I use as and when the situation requires. Depending on the situation, I may still search for new tools to manage that situation most effectively. I'm always open to different ways of doing things that serves me better.

I love coming together in groups where we discuss some of our tools – especially amongst parents or other survivors. I find there's usually much to gain from these conversations, particularly at **The Lioness Circle** where many of our black women survivors are also parents and grandparents.

By practicing these tools daily, I've gained much greater insight and control over myself which then empowered me to overcome my challenges without having to try as hard as I was a custom to.

Be open-minded

To find the right tools for you, first, you have to be open minded to trying new things and creating new habits. Also, do you have an idea of how you want to feel? Some of my women at **The Lioness Circle** create their vision board around their desired feelings. Whilst that's not a necessary part of this process, doing it could help you understand and focus more clearly on your desires.

I knew I wanted to feel increased peace and calm. I learnt this within myself from understanding what I didn't want [51] (i.e a "warzone mindset").

I also reflected on the good feelings I'd previously experienced in certain "exceptional" achievements. This included qualifying to go to one of the best High schools in Jamaica in the midst of ongoing sexual abuse and rape; and breaking many barriers as a young person in helping my family receive our permanent UK residency; and being the first person in my family to graduate from University.

Once I could acknowledge what my desired feelings felt like from these past experiences, it made it easier to guide my intentions. My aim was to go from experiencing these good feeling thoughts and emotions in exceptional cases, to intentionally creating them in me on a daily basis. This is what Abraham Hicks called 'a deliberate creator'. I wanted deliberate creation to become my norms.

I then started listening to many motivational videos including Oprah, Tony Robbins, Will Smith, Denzel Washington and many others. I felt a huge boost to my mindset and I heard a voice said, "Yes, you can!" This voice repeated over and over until I actually started believing that I could. I research other resources online and started

51 Inspired by Abraham Hicks

to attend local yoga groups; at one of them anyone could attend but the other was a specialist group for BME (Black and Minority Ethnic) women only. I'd also did some anxiety management activities with my therapist at the time – Maya Gagni - where I found breathing and meditation created the calmness I'd desired. The CBT therapy I did also helped me to better managed my thoughts, feelings and perception. I would definitely recommend Maya as a wonderful therapist to anyone who identifies their experiences similar to mine.

TIPS: The more you know what you want out of counselling or therapy, the more you're likely to gain from it. Also counselling and therapy works really well with other forms of healing such as support groups like **The Lioness Circle** and self-help/navigation tools like the ones being discussed here.

The key is to know there's a wide range of resources available both free and paid for.

Meditation was frowned upon when I was in church, although I can't remember why – except from the fear of opening up ourselves to potentially evil powers. But by this point, I'd left my religious beliefs behind because I thought that after all I'd been through, 'He' had taken all hope from me when he allowed my world to "crash" that day in my Criminal law class at University. Now I realise that was part of my victimhood mentality. That scared and wounded little girl inside me was still stuck and confused as to why she was experiencing so much pain. She tried to process and make sense of it all, but often she just couldn't, and so she escaped into her mind, blaming those responsible for her care, for what she was going through. This continued into her adult life as she regularly blamed others for her pain, including her mother and her managers.

This explains why I generally had quite negative default views of most people in authority until I later developed specific connections with some of them. I used to think some people tolerated me for reasons I didn't know, whilst others chose not to.

Fast forward to my life now, I take full accountability of my experiences and the impact they have on me, whether positive or negative. I can clearly see that my experience around breaking silent at Uni was a natural part of my 'Step 1 – Facing it' process. I don't regret it anymore, nor do I blame God or anyone else for what "happened to me". The only thing I'd change in any similar situations, is having effective tools in place to better manage such challenge.

Practising my tools

Whilst I've remained open minded and have tried many new tools, I made a list of all the ones I thought worked for me. I practiced them regularly and these became my 'new habits'. I realised within myself that if I could feel better in a split second by practicing one of these tools, imagine how I'd feel if I practiced them regularly. I'd heard in the motivational video that, "You become what you put your attention to." I wanted even more peace and calm within! I started meditating and listening to more motivational video as often as I could such as first thing in the morning, on the train to and from work, during my lunch hour and last thing before bed. Sometimes, this would be every day, but other times, life got in the way and distracted me from following this routine.

Nevertheless, I noticed lots of changes in how I managed my emotions and mental wellbeing in challenging situations. If I got stressed out at work, instead of reacting or pretending like it didn't affect me, I'd excuse myself to a private space like an empty room or toilet. I'd plug in my headphones and listen to a short-guided meditation from my phone on Youtube. At the end, I'd feel much more empowered in my mind and I'd get on with the rest of my day in good spirit, knowing I can do this again as often as I needed to. This felt much better than allowing things to build up until it explode in my mind. At home, I find myself taking deep breathes before responding to a comment or action I didn't like. By doing so, helped me to find better words of expressing myself more calmly, instead of feeling overwhelmed in my emotions, and unable to speak my truth, without shouting and trying to fight my way through. Generally, I noticed an increase sense of feeling good more times in my day, even if it was a tough day. This made me happy and proud because I knew whatever I was doing, was working.

I must point out that mastering this level took time, dedication, commitment and my willingness to seek outside of my normal habits to try new things. I say this because during this earlier stage of forming and practicing my tools (i.e. within the first 90 days), my mind was being reprogrammed, however it tried to revert back to its default settings many times even when I had the best intentions. So, it's important that everyone is aware of this and keep checking in on how different things makes them feel, in comparison to their desired feelings.

I also had to accept that what I already knew had brought me thus far, and so, in order to reach further, I needed to expand my toolbox. I had to tap into my resourcefulness. I had no idea there was so much materials available online including on Youtube and App stores which I easily accessed from my phone! My phone went from being a device I used to mainly connect with the world - to being a device that helped me connect within myself. I also had to make some tough decisions to put me first. I remember going through my turmoil at Uni where I ended up putting my needs in front of my mother's and siblings' needs; although that was so tough to do, it created the pathway for me to continue prioritizing my own needs first.

In Summary, creating new healthy habits require you to explore different self-help tools to find what works for you. It may take some time, but when you get it right, the routine created from practicing your habit, creates better mental and emotional health. It also helps us to navigate our lives more effectively. So, to create new habits:

- Know how you want to feel;
- Be resourceful and open minded to trying different tools,
- Make a list of the tools that serve your desires and
- Practice them as often as you can.

STEP 4: Reprogramming your subconscious

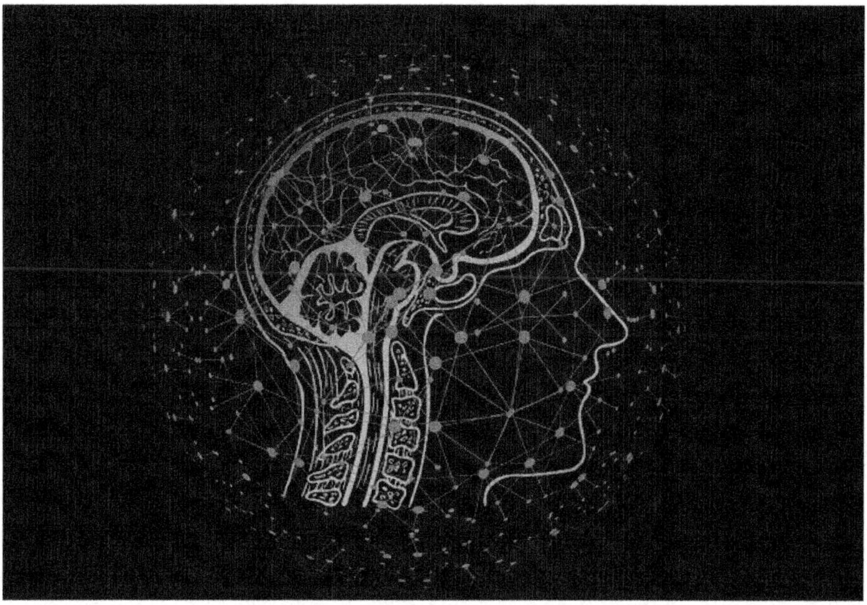

"Getting better at step 3."
Inspired by Abraham Hicks.

- Create increase space in your daily life to practice your healthy habits more often.
- Prioritize practicing your habits, just like you do for your personal hygiene.
- Be patient and kind to yourself

All the content and work we've completed through Steps 1-3, have been building you up to this point. Step 3 in particular, initiates the start of reprogramming the mind and so, at this stage, much of the foundational work is already done. Now all we need to do is to get better at practicing Step 3. Doing this will create a much deeper level of reprogramming your subconscious leading to longer periods of being in your desired state of being.

The more you're in a positive state of mind, the more tuned in you'll become to receiving guidance and support from your spirit self, including early signs of potential new challenges, as well as guidance and support of how to deal with specific situations.

Like I've noted before, challenges are a normal part of our lives. They help us to grow. The best way to handle them and receive the lessons is by catching them in the early stage and using your self-help tools to address them.

In Step 3, we used our most effective to create healthy habits. The aim of Step 4 is to prioritise the practice of these habits over a longer and more consistent period. You'll start to see a much greater shift and more benefits in repairing your mind and body – whilst connecting deeper to your spirit. I suggest you practice these for at least 90 days, although your habits should become a natural part of your ongoing routine.

Getting better at Step 3

In Step 3, we not only created new healthy habits, we also started to see some of the benefits too. Step 4 generates greater and faster impact but it requires more discipline, focus, dedication and commitment to yourself. You must decide that feeling good matters to you more than anything or anyone else. You must be committed to spending your time doing things that serves you rather than giving your attention to things that don't.

Create quality time every day to practice these tools in a safe and quiet space. However long you set aside is up to you, but it should be a minimum of 15 minutes. Whatever you do within this time should be based on the habits you've created from the tools you explored in Step 3. If you've selected a new tool to explore, it's up to you to decide the order of things during this routine.

It is ideal that you remain consistent by sticking to the same time each day, where possible. The key is trying your best and doing your best, for you. If something comes up like an urgent deadline or you overslept, try not to beat up on yourself and hold yourself at ransom! Instead, try and find a quiet time in your day to catch up on your routine. If this isn't possible, continue as normal the next day.

I embraced my habits and have allowed them to become part of my daily upkeep – similar to bathing or brushing my teeth. I thought mornings were a better time for me to practice my routine without being distracted and it would give me a better start to my day, which increased the chances of having better days. At nights, I do find it very useful to reflect on the day, identify things to celebrate and areas for development which I used in my action plan over the following days.

I used to wake up at 7am which was just enough time to get ready and leave the house. So, I decided to wake up at 5am, giving myself two hours to practice my routine (Now I wake up from 4am!) This was a huge change in my life as it meant going to bed earlier and waking up before everyone, but it has been so worth it! By making this commitment, I was also creating less time at night to gossip over the phone or watch rubbish TV, or feeling sad for some other reasons,

I not only noticed the positive differences in my thoughts and emotions each day, but I can also see myself making better decisions and managing specific challenges more effectively. In other words, "healthy habits" became a natural part of who I'd become which then reflected in my inner state of peace, calm, joy and happiness. It also projected on the external in how I better managing all areas of my life!

I started to create morning motivational live videos on my Facebook profile and chose to invest in my personal development. This included courses online and face to face, as well as having a mentor and a personal life coach. My coach was Michelle Watson, founder of Breakfree Consultancy from Overcome and Rise Above. Amongst the many things I learnt from Michelle, she taught me deeper importance of gratitude, forgiveness and celebrating my wins which have all become apart of my healthy habits too.

The more I worked on myself, the more clarity I was gaining in all areas of my life. Putting me at the centre, I'd often ask myself, "What works for me?" Sometimes, I could only figure out what I didn't want. I knew I didn't like getting into family arguments, especially those ones that goes around and round in circle; I didn't like feeling pressured or stressed out at work; I didn't like the toxic treatments in my romantic relationship, etc. From this, I worked with my coach to establish what I do want and then, I'd put them in motion.

Perfecting Step 3 enables you to tap into your Higher Power more deliberately. You'll not only feel the boost to your confidence, esteem and worth, but you'll also receive spiritual guidance. The first time you reach this level of creation within yourself, you won't want to live life any other way, ie you won't to experience negative emotions again. But remember as sure as night is to day, negative emotions are to positive ones. We no longer need to be fearful or avoid our negative feelings and emotions as we now have the right processes to manage them better.

To consciously allow the flow from your spirit, requires you to remain in a positive mindset and in the present moment. Learn to trust your intuition. Your intuition picks up guidance from your spirit and process it into your understanding. It's understandable if your intuitive system had been deeply impacted by a childhood trauma or some other experience in your adult life. The best way to get it working effectively again is to start using it again! At first, you may make some mistakes. Don't worry, this is part of your process. Take the learning points as they will help you make better decisions next time. Don't give up. Keep trying. Reflect on each message you received to try and understand more clearly if there's other interpretation you could've followed. Don't judge yourself, and don't try too hard. Just be open to keep learning and relearning about who you really are.

Be aware that your mind is likely to guide you away from anything you can't feel, taste, hear touch or smell. This is a natural reaction as the mind is programmed to keep us in our safe comfort zones. Be reminded, we're in the process of reprogramming the mind to serve us better. This is a big job and will take time to process properly. It's important that we are consciously aware of its limitations when choosing to do things differently.

The more resistance you have against this reprogramming process, the more you may even think you're going a little crazy. All of this is ok. As this is probably one of your biggest adjustment phase, try to nice and kind to yourself. Keep relying on the intuitiveness of your guidance system.

Your spirit self is always there to guide you to your true happiness. You'll see that aking the time to practice Steps 1-4, leads you straight to Step 5.

Step 5: Key to happiness

"*Being authentically you.*"

Lioness Tamar

- Boldly unmask the true you
- Be patient and kind to yourself

The fifth and final step is your highest level of Being where you are becoming the true version of yourself. By aligning your mind, body and spirit, you allow the way you feel in your body to reflect your thoughts and your thoughts to directly flow from your spirit. Through this alignment, your actions, perceptions and belief system will also synchronize to the truth that flows within you. You'll experience daily peace. Happiness will flow from inside out; even though, to others, their no apparent reason for you to be happy. You'll understand yourself better and embrace ALL of your lived experiences as you would've found greater clarity of your existence and purpose. You'll make much better decisions that serves you and your purpose. By focusing on the bigger picture to which we're all a part of, you'll release attachment to things and people around you.

Putting yourself first and prioritizing self-care will be a natural part of who you're becoming. Setting and enforcing your boundaries will also become easier. You'll stand out from the rest, and your loved ones will notice the change in you. Understand that it may take some time for others to line up to the "new" you, but don't feel like you have to change back for them or explain yourself. Chances are they won't get it. They already have a perception of you and they expect you to always fit within in. But life is not like that. We're ever growing Beings. Just know that no matter what you do, it will never please everyone. Remember everyone is at their own pace, in their own journey. Even if they don't acknowledge that, you know it, so stay in your lane!

I have no time completing with other people. My only competition is being a better me today than I was yesterday.

Birdseye view

With all that said, I do appreciate it's easier said than done. I admit that! However, it does get easier. Working through and applying the previous four steps will facilitate your growth so we can evolve to higher debts in Step 5. Whereas Steps 1-4 is about ***doing*** the inner work; learning, unlearning, relearning and creating a sustainable foundation; Step 5 is about ***allowing*** life to flow through and guiding your authentic self to the successful fulfillment of your purpose.

Another way of understanding Step 5 is by seeing Steps 1-4 as the process it takes for you to become the best solider on the battlefield with all the right armor you need to win. At Step 5, you no longer see life as a battlefield. In fact, it's become your normal way of life. You seek lessons and growth in every situation by asking: "What new lesson is this experience trying to teach me? Or "If this situation never change, what do I need to do to find peace?" I learnt those two empowering questions from Michael Bernard Beckwith's course: '***Life Visioning Mastery*** Quest' and they've proven to be exceptionally useful in receiving lessons from my challenges. Lessons give clarity, clarity gives freedom, joy and happiness.

Caution

Working your way up to stage 5 doesn't mean you won't ever dip back into Step 1 in a different time or situation. Please don't get mad or beat upon yourself when this happens. This is a normal part of the process that allows you to practice climbing through the Steps repeatedly, so you can become better and better at the climb.

When I dip back into Step 1, instead of me thinking like the victim I was, "someone is doing something to me, I now ask empowering questions like "what is trying to unfold or being born in my experience? By doing this, I'm acknowledging that challenges are normal and they help me grow. I welcome new growth and allow new wisdom and insight to reveal itself to me. Mentally coming to terms with the fact I'm no longer in an abusive situation means I no longer need to be controlled by those circumstances and I can reprogram my own mind to create new ways of dealing with challenges.

Mastery

By continuously repeating Steps 1-5 in different situations, you'll soon master the process of Overcoming Challenges 'The Lioness Way'. This will build your confidence, self-esteem and self-worth as well as deepen your beliefs and increase your trust and faith in the process. By mastering these stages, you'll know what to expect in any given situation. Even if it impacts you negatively (as we're still human, with human emotions), the main thing is that you'll be aware of the bigger picture in which each situation exists and so your response will be different to what it maybe now. You won't stay stuck or dwell in negative emotions for too long, because you know it doesn't feel good nor serve your purpose doing so. You'll find yourself naturally climbing up the Steps again, as your subconscious has now been reprogrammed this way.

You can align much of what you know now to what has always been in nature. Nature becomes our best teacher and is forever unfolding in the present moment. You may've noticed how the night changes to day, then back to night again. We don't have a breakdown over this! Even if we moan that it's too hot or too cold, we still move forward with a sense of knowing that's just how it is in this season. We accept this as part of the 'natural order of things. There's so much more we can open ourselves to learn and expand from nature, animals and everything else around us which is all necessary to continue our journey of who we really are.

Timeframe

Some people may have more resistance and barriers to overcoming each stage of 'The Lioness Way' process and so it may take them a bit longer than others to reach Step 5. That's ok, be patient, compassionate and kind to yourself. You'll find the key is not about the end result but more about the growth within the process. Trust the process. You'll soon find massive changes in the way that you respond to your environment as well as how your environment responds to you.

Final word

Mastering '***The Lioness Way***' means the Lioness has been Uncaged! She's roaring and ready for the new adventure that awaits ahead! When she takes off, she'll go with a force that no one has ever seen before!

The End (that never ends).

As I write this part of my book, I wanted to share my success of given up smoking cigarette and cannabis all at once without any help from any external factors such as a smoker's patch. I stopped drinking alcohol, again on my own. I still practice my routine every morning including exercises.

I've just completed one of Heavens Africa's 30 days Detox Gut Cleansing program, where all I've is vegetables, fruits, green juice and water. This is the first time in my life I haven't eaten a "normal" plate of food for this length of time. Even though there has been plenty of opportunities and lots of temptations, I fully surrendered to the guidance from my spirit self which has been soothing and insightful; as well as changing my relationship with food.

Life is great and I wake up happy each day completely in charge of my time and agenda. I take full accountability for what I consume and give out. I protect my vibrations and so I don't watch the news. I catch up on things of importance online. I do watch specific and beneficial programs and films when I get the chance. I balance my time with the weekly meet up group I run at **The Lioness Circle**, empowering and supporting many BAME Women survivors to rebuild their lives after domestic abuse and sexual violence (DASV), with my other group for young girls survivors. I also homeschooling my son and and I am the co-founder and one of the Directors for my community interest organisation GAGE CIC. I am a Motivational speaker, mentor, coach, DASV Practitioner and Advocate. My life is filled with many varieties and purpose driven, exactly the way I want it.

FOR THE MANY
NOT THE FEW
PEOPLE BEFORE PRIVILEGE
ab19
UKLabour
labourparty

As mentioned above, I recently spoke at the Labour Party Annual Conference 2019 in Brighton sharing my story in front of thousands of people and encouraging more women and girls' survivors to heal and get into politics and other key decision-making roles so we can be the change we want to see.

Every aspect of my life is full of so much purpose, inner happiness and I'm grateful to be driven by spiritual guidance.

WATCH NOW

Click here for video https://youtu.be/Piliptg1tHs

SUMMARY

My initial reason for writing this book was to completely release the extreme childhood challenges detailed in the first chapter of this book. It had consumed so much of my life, and created blindspots that were holding me back from becoming the person I knew deep down I was capable of becoming.

Before publishing this book, my direction changed. I found myself, not only sharing a graphic and compelling tale to my story but I was also guided to rewrite the last two chapters of the book in order to share my main strategies for overcoming challenges. This is my blueprint which I call, '***The Lioness Way***'. I trust that anyone who read this book will not only be inspired to overcome their own challenges but they may also benefit from the practical tools I've set out in the last chapter.

At first, I was resistant to sharing so much information about my personal strategies because I didn't want it to be so easily accessible. I usually only go in such details about my processes at **The Lioness Circle** or one to one with my clients. However, once I started writing it, the guidance flowed, and I found myself going in even more details than I'd expected. The idea behind this is so that more people can benefit regardless of where they're at in their journey.

Many of us are still the scared and wounded abused children - I once was – trying to seek fulfilment, joy and happiness in their lives.

The challenges I speak of in this book had disrupted my internal system from 5 years old and created so many limiting beliefs around lack and limitation which made me think of myself as worthless. By seeing myself as worthless, I was effectively showing everyone else that I was worth-less too. These negative self-beliefs impacted all areas of my life including career/business, family, romance, parenting, friendship etc. It meant I relied heavily on other people's attention and opinions to make me feel better about myself. When I didn't get what I wanted from those in my circle, I blamed them for the hurt and pain "they were causing me." When in actual fact, the hurt and pain already existed in my core and those situations were only triggering what was already there.

Without realizing this, I was trapped in a cycle of self-sabotaging behaviour, relying heavily on people and things to give me temporary satisfaction. Some of the things I relied on were drugs, alcohol, sex, binge eating, gossiping and drama, TV programs, and work. The more I lived my life this way, the more challenges I attracted, which reinforced the negative thought patterns of myself and my environment. Such as: "it's me against the world/everyone will use me if I let them in/there's no point in trying because it never works/I have to try VERY hard to get anywhere."

Feeling helpless and stuck in my situation was like being on a battlefield with nothing to defend or protect myself with; nor did I know how to escape! In fact, I'd be very defensive and hurt if anyone suggested I had the power to change my situation. It felt like they were blaming me which made me feel even worse – like they were standing there, shooting me up. This is because my mind-set was trapped in victimhood, so I couldn't perceive my situation any other way. I wasn't ready to face my past or accept responsibility for my present or future. I claimed the good times and blamed others for the bad. I also believed the good times wouldn't last long, as more bad times were right around the corner. So unbeknown to me, I was living my life on high alert waiting for the next bad thing. According to the Laws of Attraction, whatever you expect, that you shall receive.

I knew something was wrong deep down but I didn't know what it was, how to articulate it or who to talk to. In fact, for many years, I felt a huge gap inside of me. I also heard voices inside, telling me I was worth more, but there was no evidence that I could see.

I knew deep down I was capable of more, but I didn't know where to start or how to get there. I needed guidance but I was looking in all the wrong places, i.e. my mother, manager, colleagues, sisters, friends or partners. Looking in the wrong place was like banging my head against the wall then crying and complaining that it hurts. The thing is, they didn't understand what I was going through, and it was unfair to expect that anyone should.

One by one the layers piled on me, but covered with masks, it looked like I was happy and successful with so many material things around me. People overlooked my toxic ways and many wished if they had my "successful" life. But they had no idea what was really going on inside me. No one knew the scary monsters that chased me in my dreams every night or how my anxiety is was a daily struggle. And so, they couldn't help me, nor could they see how these nightmares were a symbol of my real life. No. No one knew of my ongoing depression, panic attacks or how much I relied on masks, alcohol and drugs just to cope through each day!

However, attending the University of Brighton was one of the best things I ever did! Not only did I come away with a 2:1 (LLB) Law and Business degree but as a student I also worked for Lloyds Bank which empowered me because my younger version, never thought this was ever possible.

This made me actually start to believe in myself and my capabilities that I can do anything I set my mind to, regardless of the circumstances. I was the first person in my extended family to go to University, and by doing so I inspired many younger and older family and friends to achieve more for themselves. I've been told that when people look at me, they think, "If she can do it, so can I!" Some of my younger cousins who've now been to University have told me that they were inspired by me. More importantly, going to University expanded my mindset beyond my expectations to a point where, for me to continue growing, I could no longer cover up the ***shameful*** past I'd been suppressing and burdening myself with all these years.

Having had a taste of personal success being at University, naturally I wanted more, but to reach for more, I needed to clear some of the building blocks that were in my way.

The only thing was, I was so used to wearing masks to cover up my hurt, pain and vulnerability. I didn't know when to put it down and just be my authentic self. Even if I did, would I have wanted to voluntarily give up the little happiness I was starting to enjoy in my life? After all, my masks got me through my childhood years, so why couldn't it get me through adulthood too? What evidence did I have to verify what I stood to gain in removing my masks? All I could see was what I knew - more hurt and pain. So, I held on tightly to my mask, confidently claiming it as part of who I am, until that ultimate trigger in 2007...

I was able to break my silence around childhood physical and sexual abuse as well as drug rape. Although it was very difficult getting through these challenges, I'm so grateful for the support I received from Brighton Health Services, especially the University of Brighton's counselling and GP services.

When I got married in 2012, I experienced a level of love, acceptance and safety from my marriage I'd never consciously experience before. Having my baby also in 2012 helped to bridge that gap inside me. However, I thought that getting married, having a baby and a good job would make me happy. Now that I'd done it all, I still felt the gap in me.

In 2015, I had a panic attack whilst working at FOS which resulted in me going back into therapy. This drastically increased my awareness of how I was responding to challenges, and the type of things that triggered some of my deep-rooted pain. Equipped with this knowledge I was able to identify things around me that made my situation worse whether at work, home, or elsewhere. Whilst trying to manage my triggers, I had to stay home for long periods at a time.

I was also triggered on social media after seeing one of main perpetrators, my step-dad being celebrated as a good father on Father's Day in June 2015. At this point, enough was enough. Without thinking, I "came out" by copying and posting his picture with my caption telling everyone he's a childmolester.

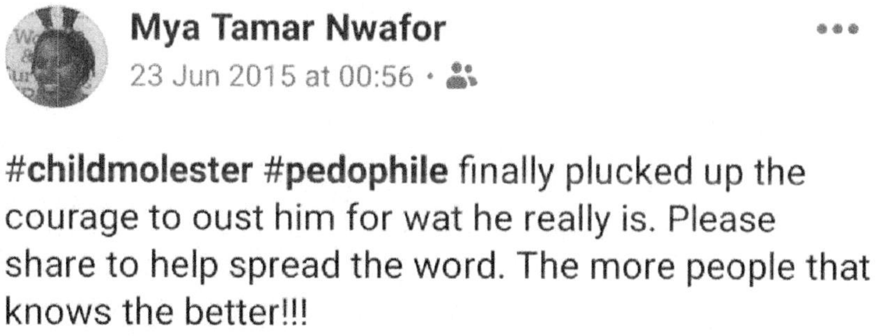
Mya Tamar Nwafor
23 Jun 2015 at 00:56 ·

#childmolester #pedophile finally plucked up the courage to oust him for wat he really is. Please share to help spread the word. The more people that knows the better!!!

This resulted in a lot of uproar amongst my family and friends who wanted to support me but also wanted me to take it down the post due to the shame and embarrassment they thought it brought on the family.

Whilst I love and respect my family, I was at a stage of putting myself first, and so having a voice and using it in this way became more important to me. To this day, the post has not been deleted from my Facebook profile.

Although I'd been through years of therapy previously, I found that breaking the silence and standing up for myself publicly in this way, took me to another level of my healing journey. I'm not saying anyone else should do it this way (it was extremely challenging), but I'm saying that by doing this, it helped ***me*** to move forward in ***my*** journey.

Since going public, I've received much love and support from online friends all over the world which empowered me inside in ways I can't even explain. I also received many messages from other survivors asking me for advice. All of these people made me feel so supported and made me actually realise I'm not alone, it's not my fault, and I had nothing to feel shameful about.

This ignited a new level of freedom, joy and happiness within me and gave me new direction for my life. One day I received a vision of myself surrounded in bright light whilst standing in front of thousands of people. At the time, I had no idea what it could be as it didn't fit in the vision of the life I'd created, which was a bit scary. I ignore it at first, then I accepted I was meant to do more. What more, I didn't know. However, my sister Joy and I set up our own community organisation called GoodAz Gold Events CIC trading as GAGE CIC. Initially we organised monthly networking events and workshops to empower our community to set up their own businesses and build generational wealth. This was important to me because I believed that my years of childhood abuse and violence was because we came from poverty and so this was my way of creating change for future generations.

I also set up Kings and Queens United Ltd in 2016 running regular workshops to equip men and women in my community to create healthier relationships.

Behind this, my marriage was breaking down and challenges hit sky high in my workplace. I started researching different forms of abuse to increase my understanding of what I'd been through and how it may still be impacting different areas of my life.

I realised I was still heavily being influenced by my childhood trauma and I needed further development support to create better changes in my life. I signed up to a number of coaching programs and online courses to develop myself. I worked on my businesses with Sharon Mclean from Business with Excellence. I also worked on myself with Michelle Watson from Breakfree Consultancy from Overcome and Rise Above.

I later went on a number of domestic abuse and sexual violence courses, and set up my own specialist self-help network for women and girls' survivors to rebuild their lives, called **The Lioness Circle**. Our ethos is 'For survivors, by survivors".

In 2018, leading up to the end of my employment at FOS, I signed up to another coaching programme with Natalie Simpson Grant. I reflected on my journey, embraced my passion, and decided to accept a huge pay cut so I could focus more of my attention on **The Lioness Circle**. Having now closed down Kings and Queens United Ltd, I recruited more directors to help me direct GAGE CIC. We decided to focus the organisation on women and girls' empowerment and expanded our services and reach of **The Lioness**

Circle - funded by local council, businesses, voluntary groups and individuals.

From the four initial black women survivors who first attended **The Lioness Circle** to over a hundred more, we have supported them in various ways. This includes one-to-one mentoring; wellbeing workshops around confidence and self-esteem, healthy relationships, overcoming challenges, vision for the future, etc; peer-to-peer support, and signposting to other local services such as counselling at the Cassandra Learning Centre. We also provide a creche, breakfast and healthy hot lunch, prepared on site each session by Lioness, chef and ambassador Heloise Ravindranath and. I found that the women were very inspired by my story, and this was a key part of why they attended and benefited from the Circle. I also empower many other women on a one to one basis, nationally.

From generational healing, to housing, employment and financial challenges, **The Lioness Circle** has been developing rapidly at the needs of it's beneficiaries. One of our key success stories was demonstrated through the emotional and practical support we gave to one of our Lionesses who successfully fought in the Family court system to get back her three children after experiencing domestic abuse in her marriage. Although funding for such well needed cause has always been a challenge, it's one we believe is well worth it.

For me, this is clear evidence that my challenges do not define me. In fact, challenges help us ALL to grow into the persons we are becoming. When we don't understand this or have the right tool to navigate our challenges, we find ourselves doing everything possible to avoid further challenges. For example, if we've been heartbroken in the past, we may avoid wanting to fall in love again. Also, as parents, if we've experienced tough challenges, we may do everything in our power to avoid our children from going through similar circumstances. The thing is, we can't run or hide from certain challenges, and by even trying to do so, we only dig ourselves deeper in the ground and drift further away from key skills and lessons necessary for our development. Although it may not seem like it during the challenge itself, later on upon reflection, the lessons always shine through. As a first time mother and a survivor of childhood sexual abuse and rape, I tried so hard to protect my son from any extreme challenges in his childhood, yet at 3 years old he experienced a traumatizing situation completely outside of my control – where he was returned into my care by the police, wet, shaking and in tears. Of course, I blamed myself for what had happened. I felt like I'd failed him and it triggered many of the negative emotions from my past. But by beating upon myself in this way, it prevented me from loving, caring and nurturing my child in the way he needed. In order to identify my child's needs and do what was right for him, I first had to make peace with myself. I had to stop beating myself up and 'Face It' which helped me to come to terms with the bigger picture: there are key lessons behind every challenge. By facing this challenge, I was able to work through my emotions and make myself available to what this challenge was trying to teach me. By repeating my own process of overcoming extreme challenges, at the time, I didn't even realise that I was creating my own blueprint!

I've now come to fully embrace that my challenges underpin the foundation blueprint of how I got from where I was to where I am. I call it: **5 Step to Overcoming Challenges: The Lioness Way.**

The Lioness Way: a 5-step process to Overcoming Challenges			
Steps	Name	Objective	Activity
STEP 1	FACE IT!	Explore the challenge - without judgement - in order to find your default pattern of responding to challenges	Thinking of a challenging situation, write down: • How did it make you feel? e.g. Angry, anxious, rejected, confused, neglected, hurt, misunderstood, deflated, etc. • What were your thoughts associated with it? • How did you react • to it (flight, flight or freeze)? • What are some of your habits associated with it? • What is your default response pattern? • What is at the core of your default response?
STEP 2	LET GO & TEK BAC YUH POWER	Let go of the hurt and pain and reclaim your power back.	Reflecting on the information shared in Step 1, write a letter to the person(s) you think have hurt you, telling them how their words and actions made you feel. Then burn the letter (or soak in water) as a symbol of letting go of the situation. Let go of the pain, hurt & blame in order to feel better, learn, grow and claim back your power.

The Lioness Way: a 5-step process to Overcoming Challenges			
Steps	Name	Objective	Activity
STEP 3	CREATE NEW HABITS	Out with the OLD, in with the NEW. Letting go of things no longer serves us, create space for things that do.	Before you start your next chapter, ensure you have effective navigation/ self-help tools in place to identify and overcome future challenges. Explore various tools such as meditation, deep breathing, journaling, visualisation, positive affirmation, prayer, gratitude, forgiveness and acceptance, mindfulness, etc. Make a list of the tools that works for you, and use them to create health habits which you'll pratice as often as you can.
STEP 4	REPROGRAM YOUR SUBCON-SCIOUS	Getting better at step 3.	Be kind to and look after yourself. Set aside time each day to regularly practice your healthy habits so they become a normal part of who you are. Keep practicing!
STEP 5	KEY TO HAPPINESS	Be authentically you!	Make a commitment to yourself to create a healthier and more balanced relationship with your spiritual self. Practice putting yourself first. Try it. It feels AMAZING!

'***The Lioness Way***' has been inspired by the teaching of the Law of Attraction from a number of modern-day teachers such as Abraham Hicks, Lisa Nichols and Michael Beckwith. It has been successfully tried and tested at **The Lioness Circle** as well as my individual clients. As I write this, my women and girls of **The Lioness Circle** have been working with Cezanne Taharqa, an author and poet, to write an anthology as they've become increasingly passionate about breaking their silence publicly and sharing their stories with the world.

From the abused and battered little girl to reaching personal success and using this to empower many other women and girls, I find myself growing from strength to strength each day. If you think my story is unique, you're right. But we all have unique stories. We're all on our own individual journeys going at different paces. Challenges are a natural part of this journey. None of us are perfect, and we all need support at one stage or another.

One in four of us will experience some form of mental health at some stage in our lives.

One in three women and girls worldwide will experience some form of either physical or sexual violence in their lifetime. [52] This figure doesn't even consider other forms of domestic abuse such as physiological, coercive control, financial abuse, harassment or digital abuse. Click here for more information about the different types of abuse. [53] It also doesn't consider the many more unreported cases.

Many women and girls who're affected by mental health could be as a result of domestic abuse and sexual violence, but it could also

52 https://www.who.int/news-room/fact-sheets/detail/violence-against-women
53 https://www.womensaid.org.uk/information-support/what-is-domestic-abuse/

be as a result of countless other challenges in life. Too many of us (including men) are suffering in silence, unable to cope, resulting in suicide. We must choose to support each other instead of trying to compete with or control each other. Getting the right support when we need it can make such a huge difference in how we manage our challenges and navigate our life more effectively.

That scared little girl is now living a life of inner peace, joy and happiness. It doesn't mean my life is perfect, but what it does mean is that I live my life in the fun and enjoyment that each moment unfolds – giving me greater clarity, purpose, and context of my existence. I understand my purpose and how my purpose contributes to the higher purpose. I allow life to flow through me in how I perceive and experience it, rather than being confined or controlled by external factors.

This book shows where my journey into this life started. What I want my readers to know is that these extreme challenging circumstances was only the beginning. It was like laying the foundation. Imagine building a house; before it's completed and decorated, there's a lot of hard labour that must be included. Certain parts must happen before others can begin, and if we try to rush it (e.g. before the cement dries), the whole thing can crumble. Well this is similar to building/creating our lives. These challenging experiences are a natural part of laying the bricks which must be done before we can flow with it and enjoy it. I'm not saying it's easy, but you can do it, with the right support and tools you need to navigate your life.

Once you've mastered '***The Lioness Way***' you'll be in a much better position to create your own blueprint too. You'll not only become the CEO of managing and navigating your own life, you'll also become a valuable asset in your community. Others will see something in you and want to be guided by your wisdom.

Rise up Lionesses, the time to Uncage is now. ***ROAR!***

Life is constantly expressing itself through me and it's doing it through you too. In fact, I know many of my readers may be going through tough challenges and could benefit from some additional support. If this sounds like you or someone you know, see the list below for some of the services available in the UK. Alternatively, please search online for other services in your local area.

Now that the Lioness has been Uncaged, what next? What kind of adventure awaits? Will she continue to thrive on her journey ahead? Watch out for my next book which I'm currently writing, and should be out it in the next 12 months. Watch this space...

Self-soothing/ being kind

- ✓ Acknowledge things feel difficult
- ✓ Light a scented candle or oils
- ✓ Bring air into your home, open windows
- ✓ Write at least one page in your journal of thoughts you may want to dump
- ✓ Place a small pebble/ object that is special to you in your pocket or bag
- ✓ Make your bed with care so when you are ready to rest it is waiting for you
- ✓ Let yourself know that you are taking care as much as you can
- ✓ Have a bath put bubbles/ scent in especially for you
- ✓ Say 'NO', every time you can say NO to something you do not want to do. You are saying YES to your selfcare and what you need
- ✓ Write a supportive comforting letter to the small part of you
- ✓ If you are shopping swap an item for one thing you like that is healthy
- ✓ Tell yourself that you are entitled to feel as you do – it is a NORMAL reaction to abnormal experiences
- ✓ Spend an extra 15 minutes with your pets
- ✓ Try and drink one extra glass of water
- ✓ Cream or oil your skin/ hands and face – take time and acknowledge your own kindness
- ✓ Wear a comforting piece of clothing/shoes etc
- ✓ Watch a programme or feel good film
- ✓ If you can, tell a safe person that you are struggling today, this week
- ✓ Replace one hour of social media with reading a magazine or book or listen to an audio book
- ✓ Prepare or cook a meal that you enjoy
- ✓ Tell yourself you are braving these feelings and you are going to try your best to be kind to yourself until it passes
- ✓ Try to eat at meal times- even something small if it is a struggle or try a healthy drink
- ✓ Put your feet into soapy water for 10 minutes, dry them and cream them
- ✓ Look through photos of healthy happy memories in your life
- ✓ Write one page in your journal of where you would like to be in a years' time in your recovery- be as positive as you like!
- ✓ Let yourself rest but also try one thing from this list before your rest and after
- ✓ Book a massage or take 20 minutes to massage your own feet and hands- use cream or oil
- ✓ Listen to your favourite music artist or listen to meditation
- ✓ Drive to an area/ place where you like the scenery
- ✓ Have a walk or run and acknowledge how being active is important to help your brain work
- ✓ Sing out loud in your car or home
- ✓ Call a helpline for support- Samaritan's. you deserve to be supported
- ✓ Punch a pillow and acknowledge you have feelings you deserve to release
- ✓ At the end of the day before you shut your eyes acknowledge with warmth that you have struggled and that you are going to hold yourself with kindness every step that you can

**Once your emotions have settled. Make a note of what you did to get through and add to your emergency tool kit/box for the next time. Remember it takes time and practice, sitting with distress takes immense courage!*

10 Top tips: How to increase your self-confidence:

1) Becoming more insightful and reflective through mindfulness practices lead to greater awareness of our own limiting beliefs that affects our self- esteem and confidence.

2) We must make a conscious decision to let go of or stop judgements and limiting beliefs. Every time we become aware of them, move into a space of self-acceptance and positivity. This includes our own self-judgements and what other people think. We may even need to review our circle to remove those that don't contribute to our lives in a positive way.

3) Seeking to understand and accept, rather than judge and dismiss can be a more caring way to show love to ourselves and others. This is applicable even if we hated someone in the past or hated something about ourselves.

4) Get out of our comfort zone! Confidence begins at the edge of our comfort zone so we need to try stretching ourselves. Try something new, meet new people or try to view a situation from a different perspective or approach.

5) Mastering particularly experiences or a new skill that compliments who we are or what we want to do can increase our confidence and self-belief and thus being capable of accomplishing what we want in the future.

6) Don't hold ourselves to unrealistic standards and goals then expect them to quickly transform our lifelong habits. Be proud and gentle on ourselves as we embark on a long and challenging journey of self-discovery and self-acceptance.

7) Take a moment and reflect on (and write down) all the things we've achieved especially when we'd initially thought we couldn't. We could even elaborate on why we felt proud of those accomplishments. Use the list as a reminder of our abilities when we need a little boost.

8) Use our talents, skills and abilities to help someone/others. For example, give someone direct assistance, share helpful resources, teach someone something they want to learn or offer something we do well as a gift to someone.

9) Heal from our past! Unresolved issues and drama can keep us trapped in low-self-esteem. Get counselling and/or join a support groups like the Lioness Circle, so we can get assistance to heal and move on from our past.

10) Create new and healthy habits that encourages us to read/listen/watch daily inspirational materials that uplifts us and make us feel positive about ourselves. Start searching on YouTube now!

10 Top tips to creating healthier relationships:

1) **Love yourself:** Being comfortable with who you are means you'll be a happier partner.

2) **Communicate**: Talk to the other person in the relationship. Ask questions and listen to their answers. If you're upset, say so, don't make the other person have to try and figure it out. And making negative comments doesn't help to build healthy relationships. Talking through issues build trust and make your relationship stronger. Also don't forget to let them know when they do something that makes you happy.

3) **Be Honest**: Be truthful with each other about what you do, think and feel. Honesty comes from trust. Lies can create toxic environments and ruin relationships.

4) **Set Boundaries:** Setting personal boundaries and standards is a mark of a truly mature person. Talk this over with the other person, ideally from the beginning of the relationship. What are certain things you will and won't accept or do? A lack of boundaries invites a lack of respect.

5) **Give each other some space**: Spending time with the other person is great, but spending ALL of your time with the other person isn't great! It's healthy to have your own friends, interests and other relationships outside of a specific relationship to rely on and to create fulfilment.

6) **Keep Social Media out of your relationship:** when it comes to problems in your relationships, keep social media out of it. Don't post negative comments online. Your Facebook, Instagram, Snapshot or Twitter friends don't need to know or get involve!

7) **Agree to Disagree**: You're not always going to see eye to eye, and that's OK. The important thing is to respect each other's opinion and ideas. Everybody make mistakes. Be willing to apologise for yours – and accept the other person's apology.

8) **Support each other**: When the other person does something great, tell them! They should also tell you when you do something great too! It's important to know you won't be able to support each other 100% of the time. This is because of many reasons such as your own individual challenges or distance in the relationship and that's ok. Having a specific person in your life because you completely depend on them is not healthy and unlikely to end well. Talk to the other person so that you both understand this.

9) **Talk about sex... openly and honestly**: In an intimate relationship, tell the other person what feels good and what you like or don't like – helps make the sex better. Never pressure the other person into doing something they don't want and don't let anyone pressure you either – **consent** is a must!

10) **Take care of your sexual health**: Talk to the other person about how you're going to protect each other against STD's and unintended pregnancy. Practice safe sex and get regular check ups.

Dedication from The Lioness Circle

““The moment I re-discovered my value, my price range went up significantly to PRICELESS! And from that day on, I declined any offers that was less than.”

Heaven Africa

“You’re the most beautiful queen I have ever seen and with the most special heart that some people may abuse but you will survive and thrive in life because love conquers all. As long as u r 100% real and accepting of who you are, true happiness will shine upon you.”

Kimberley Jones

“From the depths of my being I salute and appreciate you and my Sisters’ for being a genuine Lioness-a voice for us thrivers!”

Gracie

“Tamar, thank you for sharing your story and inspiring us to move forward and embrace life with renewed sight. Forever grateful x”

Anonymous

“From my first day this has been a safe space for me. Such powerful energy, you remind us Lionesses its our choice to give our selves **permission to shine!**”

Anonymous

“Since I’ve gone to the group, I’ve flourished being around such positive woman. Tamar has shown me when you’ve hit your lowest the only way you can go is up.”

Anonymous

Phenomenal women. Keep Rising !

Steph Lindo

From Negativity to positivity, I now have creativity
leading to tranquillity."

Joanna-S'healing

THANKS

Let me take this opportunity to thank myself for doing the inner work and be able to share my truth with everyone else. I not only wrote this book myself but I also edited parts of it too.

I send lots of love, peace and joy to everyone who has contributed to my life, as it's all helped me to become the person I am today. I smile as I write this because I love the person who I've become and I wouldn't have wanted it any other way. Every day new lessons and blessings unfolds, giving me greater insight and meaning to my life which is all taking me closer to the fulfilment of my life's purpose in this physical form. Through this way of being, the Universe is constantly providing me evidence of my happiness, reflecting back to me where I am. You've all been apart of my journey and for that I'll always be grateful.

Special thank you to my family and friends all over the world including my mother, father, sisters, brothers, my Prince Zion and his father, niece, nephews, cousins, grand aunts, uncles and grand uncles, grandfather and grandmother.

I also thank my therapist, mentors, coworkers, business partners and all the women and girls from **The Lioness Circle**.

To everyone else in the community who have directly or indirectly contributed to my work and my journey, whether to my consciousness or not.

Thank you to everyone who has and will support this book. By doing so, you're not only benefiting from the contribution it will have our your journeys, but you're also raising money towards **The Lioness Circle**'s specialist support group for BME women and girls' survivors of domestic abuse and sexual violence.

Taking My Power Back, by: Lioness Tamar

I'm taking my power back from everything and everyone that I'd given a slice. It was always mine to take back, but I didn't realise this, until now.

From the childhood molester, to the prevented teacher, controlling boyfriend, friendimies, and countless situations where I felt

too dumb to even utter a single word. From drugs, alcohol and everything in between.

You see, in the past I gave it up blindly, and so easily - over and over again, leaving me helpless in the midst of the storm.

But now I've travelled the path and have awoken to this, I'm taking my power back.

I can feel the ancestors and descendants celebrating in this moment.

It's mine. It's my birth right. My identity.

It's a bundle of unique gifts, talents, and other possibilities to navigate life in a way that not only fulfils my purpose, but it serve the expansion of humanity too.

It's the creator within me.

Me without my power is like a microwave without electricity - useless.

It's time I become the person I came here to be.

The powerful Goddess that shines it's brightness and awakes the world to the goodness that lives in you, me, and all of us. And this starts with taking my power.

I'm not saying there won't be other challenges where I might slip and drip my power in the waste again, because that's what I'm used to do.

What I am saying is that I now realise those old habits no longer serve me, so, I'm kicking them to the kerb.

I'm creating new habits.

I'm, taking my power back!

You Don't See Me, by: Lioness Tamar

You don't see me, not in the way I see you.

You don't see me and I don't blame you coz I don't see me too.

You don't see me or how hard I've tried to get your attention.

No, I don't mean seeing what I do or say. Or you looking upon my pretty face, bright eyes, big thighs, ass, hips or tits when you want something from me.

No, I'm talking about the me inside me.

She's been longing for your attention. To be acknowledged. To be accepted and understood.

To be normal, noticed, nurtured. To experience real love. What IS real love?

Not knowing how to give her what she needs is driving me crazy, literally!

Sometimes it's like a warzone in my mind, running and screaming, fears and escape –

Except there's no escape. So, I stop running, and stand there with my arms at my side taking all the bullets until I finally drop to the ground.

With all this going on inside me, no wonder why I feel so weird, certainly different to everybody else.

Somehow, I've convinced myself that it's my fault. So, I cover it up with a smile

I carry around on my face so no one will judge or blame me for what I must have done to myself.

I don't think I could handle THAT too; it could just be the tipping point.

Who can I talk to about this? No one.

So, I try to pretend like this isn't happening, like she's not hurting, in pain, reliving past traumatic experiences over and over again.

But she won't let me forget. Every now and then someone or something ignites her again, or was it something in the air? I can't always remember what triggers her off - but whenever she takes over, the entire life that I've built falls right to the ground; and I can't predict what's gonna happen next 'coz I don't know what she's really capable of.

I have tried to shut her up permanently, but not even that I'm capable of doing without her say so.

Now I just try to cope the best way I can, living in the same body as her.

After 34 years you'd think I'm used to it, right?! Wrong!

All I do is find more and more ways of shutting her up.

Like finding various distractions to obsess about, not healthy respectful things my mother would be proud of. No. I mean living life dangerously on the edge. I called it drugs, sex and crime.

The stronger the drugs and alcohol, the easier it is to enjoy this kind of life without her interruptions.

In fact, I can always count on Mr Wray and his nephew to get the job done!

So even if you'd met her, you probably wouldn't have noticed her.

No. No one can see her until I see her. Until I feel her, hear her, listen to her, acknowledge her, embrace her. Learn to love her. Besides she'll never be happy with anything less and I can't truly experience this with anyone else before her.

So, at 34, I'm learning new ways of life. This time, it's not to run from her or even shut her up. No. This time, it's to FREE her, because freeing her frees me too.

Yes, I see her, for the first time in my life, I don't need you or anyone else to acknowledge.

Making her happy is making me the happiest I've ever been, and it's not just temporary.

You see we're now on this journey together figuring out why we're both here.

And she's so much fun, I think we could be best friends for life.

They say life begins at 40, but I guess at 34, my real life has just begun!

OTHER RESOURCES

Domestic abuse or violence is a crime and should be reported to the police - there are also other organisations who can offer you help and support.

Call 999 if it's an emergency or you're in immediate danger.

The police take domestic violence seriously and will be able to help and protect you.

Contact your local neighbourhood policing team if it's not an emergency.

Other organizations who can help

Contact any of the following organisations to get help and advice about domestic abuse.

Freephone National Domestic Abuse Helpline, run by Refuge
0808 200 0247 www.nationaldahelpline.org.uk

The Family Justice Centre
020 8688 0100 helpline
c@croydon.gov.uk

Galop (for lesbian, gay, bisexual and transgender people)
0800 999 5428
www.galop.org.uk

Men's Advice Line
0808 801 0327
www.mensadviceline.org.uk

Rape Crisis (England and Wales)
0808 802 9999
www.rapecrisis.org.uk

Scotland's Domestic Abuse and Forced Marriage Helpline
0800 027 1234
sdafmh.org.uk

Scottish Women's Aid
0131 226 6606
www.scottishwomensaid.org.uk

Wales Domestic Abuse Helpline

0808 80 10 800

www.allwaleshelpline.org.uk

Women's Aid Federation (Northern Ireland)
0800 917 1414
www.womensaidni.org

Women's Aid (England)
info@womensaid.org.uk
www.womensaid.org.uk

The Survivor's handbook gives you all your basic information you need to understand around domestic abuse including what it is and how to get help. To access it, visit Women's Aid website: www.womensaid.org.uk/the-survivors-handbook/

Black and Minority Ethnic (BME) Survivors

The Lioness Circle: a peer to peer self-help support network for BME women and girls' survivors of domestic abuse and sexual violence. Created for us and by us, it empowers survivors to rebuild their lives after abuse and violence. It provides mentoring, wellbeing workshops, coaching, signposting, emotional support, breakfast, lunch, creche and much more.

Lionesstamar.com
Tamar@lionesstamar.com
07904875793

Women's Aid: more information is available for Black, Asian or minority ethnic women trying to escape from domestic abuse at www.womensaid.org.uk/the-survivors-handbook/womenfrom-bme-communities/

Most of the information above and more can be found on the UK gov official site: https://www.gov.uk/report-domestic-abuse. If you're living in another country and would like additional support, please check your government's website or the internet for what's available in your area.

Printed in Great Britain
by Amazon

18674643R10163